CAREERS
in Criminology

CAREERS in Criminology

Marilyn Morgan

ROXBURY PARK

LOWELL HOUSE

LOS ANGELES

NTC/Contemporary Publishing Group

Library of Congress Cataloging-in-Publication Data

Morgan, Marilyn (Marilyn D.)
    Careers in criminology / by Marilyn Morgan
    p. cm.
    Includes bibliographical references and index.
    ISBN 0-7373-0272-0 (alk. paper)
        1. Criminal justice, Administration of—Vocational guidance— United
    States. 2. Criminology—Vocational guidance—United States. I. Title.

    HV9950 . M674 2000
    364'.023'73—dc21   99-52535

Published by Lowell House
A division of NTC/Contemporary Publishing Group, Inc.
4255 West Touhy Avenue, Lincolnwood (Chicago), Illinois 60712-1975 U.S.A.

Lowell House books can be purchased at special discounts when ordered in bulk
for premiums and special sales. Contact Department CS at the following address:

NTC/Contemporary Publishing Group
4255 West Touhy Avenue
Lincolnwood, IL 60712-1975
1-800-323-4900

Roxbury Park is a division of NTC/Contemporary Publishing Group, Inc.

Managing Director and Publisher: Jack Artenstein
Editor in Chief, Roxbury Park Books: Michael Artenstein
Director of Publishing Services: Rena Copperman
Editor: Rachel Livsey
Managing Editor: Nicole Monastirsky
Interior Designer: Andrea Reider

Printed and bound in the United States of America
        6 7 8 9 0   DSH/DSH   0 1 0 9 8 7

CONTENTS

THE WORLD OF CRIMINAL JUSTICE HAS BEEN A CENTRAL FOCUS of my life for nearly thirty years. In 1970, policing in America was, in many respects, at a crossroads. The country was being torn apart by civil unrest fueled by the civil rights movement and opposition to America's involvement in Vietnam, and the police were caught squarely in the middle. Part of the population viewed them as a guardian force protecting the country from lawless demonstrators while others perceived them as an occupying force.

It was also during this time that the federal legislation that developed out of the President's Report on Crime in America (1967) began to make itself felt. Police officers were being hired in record numbers and urban police departments were growing rapidly in size. Huge sums of money were channeled into secondary-education programs aimed at raising the educational level of U.S. police officers.

It was during this period of conflict and change that I drifted into municipal policing. It was an exciting time to enter this dynamic occupation, particularly for a young man who had spent most of his life in a rural setting prior to joining a big-city police department. I was the kind of person who would have profited from this book.

I have worked as a uniformed patrol officer, plainclothes officer, public information officer to three chiefs of police, patrol sergeant, crime prevention supervisor, academy instructor, detective sergeant in sexual assault and child abuse investigations, and operations and liaison sergeant to an assistant chief of police. I have participated in hundreds of oral boards for police officer candidates and have participated in the promotional assessment centers for various police departments. I was part of a national search for the chief of police of the small town in which I live and am a commissioner on that town's Public Safety Commission. And finally, when I retired from policing, I took a teaching position in the field of criminal justice.

With this background in criminal justice, I recognize the value of a book on careers in criminology. This book identifies a wide variety of the different kinds of jobs available in criminal justice. Few people are aware of the opportunities available for the studious type with strengths in the sciences who can reconstruct skeletal remains or painstakingly lift fingerprints from impossible surfaces. Of the more than 1.5 million jobs available in criminal justice, the possibilities are endless: from police officer to county sheriff to federal agent to polygrapher to forensic specialist to trial attorney, this book helps direct the uninitiated in the right direction. It provides starting points, discusses common starting salaries, and covers general education requirements. It provides a good introduction for persons considering careers in criminal justice.

A highlight of this book is the inclusion of anecdotal information from working professionals in the field, all highly regarded professionals nationally and in some cases internationally. One truth I have learned in life is to listen to the voice of experience, whether it is one's own or someone else's. Experience is the foundation of true learning and those considering this line of work can learn much by listening to the voices in this book.

The field of criminal justice continues to evolve with society and advances in technology. It has been said that mankind has learned more in the last fifty years than in all of previous recorded history. My experience tells me that unless a way is found to eradicate crime altogether, there will continue to be ample employment opportunities in this field well into the next millennium. The first criminal code was written during the Babylonian period more than 4,000 years ago. With crime yet to be eradicated it is a safe bet that this less-than-profound prediction will hold true. Marilyn Morgan's book clearly demonstrates the possibilities that exist in a profession directed toward the goal of eradicating crime.

LEE LIBBY

Professor of Criminal Justice
Shoreline Community College
Shoreline, Washington

ACKNOWLEDGMENTS

T HERE ARE MANY PEOPLE I NEED TO THANK WHO HELPED ME in myriad ways with the writing of this book.

To Deputy U.S. Marshal Dennis Behrend, who helped me immensely and made my job easier. He was a valuable advisor who went out of his way to assist with interviews, contacts, and materials.

To retired Captain Michael Nault of the Seattle Police Department and U.S. Marshal Rosa Melendez, who allowed me to interview them and introduced me to other people in the industry.

To public affairs officials Mike Sampler of the Secret Service, Neal Schiff of the Federal Bureau of Investigation (FBI), and especially David Braham of the Marshals Service who took the time and effort to help me gather information and photographs.

To Jeff Geoghagan, Seattle police officer, and Tito Del Valle and Brian Morgan, deputy marshals, who allowed me to ask questions and observe their training sessions.

To all the people who took time out of their busy schedules to allow me to interview them, including King County Sheriff David Reichert, Bellevue Chief of Police James Montgomery, Major Fabienne Brooks of the King County Sheriff's Department, FBI agent Marita Malone, forensic scientist Kay Sweeney, attorneys Theresa Olson and Mark Larson, correction specialist Patricia Scholes, Sergeant Steven Davis of the King County Sheriff's Department, chief of staff Moses Ector of the Georgia Bureau of Investigation, security specialist Ron Edwards, Gary Lark of the Escanaba, Michigan Department of Safety, and retired officer Mark Hurley of the San Francisco Police Department.

To all from Automated Fingerprint Identification Service (AFIS) in the King County Sheriff's Department who provided invaluable information, including regional AFIS manager Marilyn Nault, Wade Petroka, Michael French, and Cassandra Sonnenberg.

To Professor Lee Libby, who provided me with tons of valuable information.

And special thanks to Laura O'Hare for her invaluable assistance in the research, development, and writing of the final draft of this manuscript.

W HEN I SET OUT TO WRITE THIS BOOK I WAS VERY EXCITED at the prospect—I have always been intrigued with criminal justice. I rarely miss an episode of *The Practice* or *Law & Order.*

In my opinion *Law & Order* is an accurate depiction of the justice process, from the commission of the crime to the police investigation to the suspect's arrest and prosecution, as well as all the dealings and politics that occur outside of the courtroom.

The topic of this book, criminal justice, is defined as those aspects of social justice that concern violations of the criminal law, and the law enforcement activities and court procedures that deal with the violators and enforce those laws. The criminal justice system is defined as the combination of all aspects of the operational, administrative, and technical divisions needed to carry out criminal justice functions.

During my years as a reporter I spent a great deal of time covering two particular "beats" related to criminal justice: the police and the courthouse. I had the opportunity to get to know many professionals working in law enforcement and the court system. I had many long discussions with them about their careers and learned what drew them to their professions and why they enjoyed them.

When I began to decide what would be included in this book, I knew that one of my most important objectives was to offer real insight into what these jobs are like. To that end, I interviewed and profiled some of the top professionals in the field of criminal justice. As Professor Lee Libby, director of criminal justice at Shoreline Community College, states in his foreword, some of those profiled have national and even international reputations, making their experiences and advice invaluable to anyone thinking of embarking on a career in criminology.

My second goal was to present a comprehensive look at the careers available in criminal justice. Accordingly, I discuss professional functions and duties, the qualifications necessary to apply for the jobs, and the training required to join the profession. Not all the careers discussed here involve being a sworn officer; many of the vital roles in criminal justice, such as forensic and computer specialists, are performed by civilians. Not all the careers discussed here involve being a sworn officer; many of the vital roles in criminal justice, such as forensic and computer specialists, are performed by civilians.

This book covers the major aspects of the criminal justice systems. From the law enforcement officers on the street, to crime-scene specialists, the courts, the prison system, and private security, this vast system offers a variety of careers.

Careers in law enforcement and criminal justice are interesting, challenging, and growing. There are more than 17,000 local police departments and seventy major federal law enforcement agencies. Prosecutors and criminal-defense lawyers hold more than 600,000 positions and judges more than 78,000, while 320,000 people are employed in corrections. It's clear from these numbers that the criminal justice system has grown, and according to the Bureau of Labor Statistics, the field will continue to grow at a faster rate than all other professions.

The education requirements for these careers can be as varied as the careers themselves. As an example, some college experience is generally sufficient to become a police detective, whereas a bachelor's degree is needed to become a FBI special agent.

Minimum requirements aside, many departments encourage their officers to seek a degree in criminal justice, and statistics indicate that the trend is toward requiring post-high-school education. The study of criminal justice includes courses in criminal law, ethics, and police organization and administration, and aids students in developing necessary skills such as leadership, analytical reasoning, and communication. These skills are important for pursuing any career, but are particularly vital to the ones discussed in this book.

The opportunities in criminal justice are nearly endless. It's my hope and intention that this book offers information the reader needs to begin pursuing these opportunities, along with an interesting and accurate portrayal of work in the criminal justice field.

PART ONE

Officers on the Front Lines

A N OFFICER APPROACHES A CLOSED DOOR, NOT KNOWING whether what waits behind it is an empty room or a suspect whose gun will be pointed straight at her; an FBI agent uncovers a piece of the psychological puzzle that leads him to a brutal rapist; a detective's days of interrogation pay off when a drug carrier reveals his boss and a major supplier is taken off the streets. In another part of the country, the president of the United States walks safely through a crowd as the Secret Service keeps a watchful eye; a U.S. marshal retrieves a cell-phone call that leads to the fugitive he's been tracking for months; a sheriff's deputy works the computer, pretending to be a young girl, and lures an on-line pedophile to a meeting that will send the predator to jail, safely away from the children he stalks.

These are just a few of the challenges faced each day by "the front lines" of law enforcement—the officers, agents, and deputies who come face to face with criminals either helping a community pull together, or intervening when it tries to tear itself apart.

What qualities does it take to work in this world? There are many, including common sense, courtesy, and a sense of community obligation; intelligence; a keen awareness of your surroundings; the ability to act when necessary but know when to refrain; education; special training; and a well-rounded knowledge of your field and those that relate to it.

For those who choose careers in law enforcement, the rewards of helping people, saving lives, and keeping a community safe are balanced with the difficulties of long hours, stressful conditions, and sometimes frustrating or dangerous situations.

In the first section of this book, these "front line" careers in law enforcement are examined to help you consider whether they could represent the career for you.

CHAPTER ONE

The Community's First Line of Defense

Uniformed Officers

DURING THE COURSE OF A DAY, ONE MAN WILL SPEAK TO A room full of grade-school children about the dangers of drugs; two women will intervene in a domestic violence dispute, eventually leading a brutal man off to jail and initiating the process that sends the woman and her children to a shelter and safety; a man and a woman on bicycles will cruise a family neighborhood, keeping sidewalks clear of loiterers and making it safe and easy for the neighbors to shop, walk, and conduct the business of their day.

Oddly enough, the people doing these seemingly very different jobs all have the same job title: uniformed police officer.

■ OFFICERS ON THE BEAT

Uniformed officers do their jobs from a variety of posts: on foot, in patrol cars, on horseback and bicycle, in motor boats and air patrols. Some are fresh out of the police academy and some are twenty-year veterans. They are of every race and nationality, and both men and women are valued for the skills they bring to the job. What they share is commitment to community, an ability to communicate and work with the public, the training to keep their cool and concentrate during the worst possible situations, and a willingness to put their lives on the line on a daily basis.

The variety of an officer's daily activity is linked in part to the size of his or her police department. Small-town police officers respond to a variety of neighborhoods—commercial and residential, well-to-do, and lower-income. They could be dealing with a neighbor's dispute over a missing morning paper one minute or a jewelry store robbery the next. In midsize or large police departments, the officers have specific areas of patrol, known as "beats." Each beat has its own problems, whether they be the frustrations of language and cultural barriers in an immigrant neighborhood or the demanding attitude of wealthy residents who see the public servants as their own private force. Although certain crimes may be more common in certain communities, it's important for an officer to avoid assumptions about what's happened based on the economic or cultural makeup of the participants involved. As recent news events have emphasized over and over again, domestic violence, murder, and child abuse do not discriminate.

▒ TWO OVERVIEWS ON POLICING

Officer Gary Lark of the Escanaba, Michigan Department of Safety (a combined policing and firefighting department) and retired officer Mark Hurley of the San Francisco Police Department (who still works regularly counseling fellow officers on financial and other matters) have a lot in common: a love of their communities, a smart and thoughtful approach to the work they do, and a real commitment to their fellow officers. What differs is the size of the communities they serve, and the problems and opportunities afforded each by their chosen work environment.

Law Enforcement in Small Towns

Escanaba, Michigan, is a small city of 12,500 whose primary businesses are the paper mill and machine parts factory. While Escanaba's middle income is lower than the national average, recent generations have enjoyed a steady low of 6 percent unemployment even during the recent recession of the 1990s. "We're consistent here," laughs Lark, who grew up in Escanaba. "We're about as consistent a community as you could possibly find."

Lark's department is part of the Delta County law enforcement community, which links the Escanaba station with others such as Burke River (population 1,200) and Gladstone (population 4,500), the Delta County sheriff's department, and the state police. Although Lark could have worked in the Detroit police force, he chose to stay in Escanaba. "When I graduated from North Michigan University, the Escanaba department was really becoming progressive . . . we had a good chief and I felt I could make a real difference."

The first important program Lark was involved in was one of safety. "People were burning wood fires everywhere and we were getting four or five blazes a day. We instituted an education program and that number dropped almost immediately. Then we went after building owners, tore down low-rent housing being leased to transient teenagers, and made landlords come in and clean up. This stopped the majority of the building fires. We rarely have a problem now."

Seasonal problems aren't limited to fires. "Assaults and domestic crimes are a real problem up here. There's still a lot of what I'd call a 'logging mentality' in the way people deal with each other." In the winter, people are trapped indoors for much of the time. "If there's a problem, it's not like they can take a walk around the block to cool off," notes Lark.

Lark's current assignment keeps him closely involved with the personal lives of the community; for the past four years he has worked as the department's school liaison. "I have a regular schedule," Lark explains. "Mornings I go to the junior high, later the high school. I take reports about problems with students and school property thefts . . . the job is the same for all the schools, but the problems are bigger with the high school." Lark is involved whether the problem started at school or was recognized there. That means if a student is on drugs, or the possible victim of physical or sexual abuse at home, Lark is there. "It definitely makes it easier for kids to tell me things because I'm around all the time. It was a gradual thing, kids being willing to come forward and trust me." Lark cements that relationship by coaching the Community High football team, a role he's enjoyed for the past fifteen years. "It's important to be a part of the community." He and his fellow officers in every branch of Delta County law enforcement further that commitment with charity events that sponsor youth groups, drug- and alcohol-free dances and graduation parties, and other positive youth activities. "You don't want to just be there when things go wrong," Lark says. "You want to be a positive role model."

Big City Police Departments

Retired police officer Mark Hurley also chose the hometown force, in his case the San Francisco Police Department. Hurley was an active member of the department for thirty years and still works with its Widows and Orphans Fund and volunteers for everything from cooking for department get-togethers to sponsoring an annual St. Patrick's Day event that supports the Police Athletic League (PAL), a popular and well-established youth program.

Hurley joined the force in the 1960s, when competition for jobs was fierce. Weekly classes taught by working and retired officers cost fifty cents and were conducted in an instructor's basement.

After years as a patrol officer, Hurley was appointed head of animal control by Mayor Joseph Alioto, a post that brought him in contact with the victim of one of the most notorious crimes in San Francisco history, supervisor Harvey Milk.

Harvey Milk became the nation's first openly gay politician when he was elected to the San Francisco Board of Supervisors in 1977. Milk received broad support as a human-rights activist who was passionate about care of the elderly and worked to improve the city's quality of life. One of the laws he passed, written with Hurley, was the city's first "pooper-scooper" statute, which required dog owners to clean up after their pets. According to Hurley, "these kinds of quality-of-life laws make a real difference in a city. When you start letting things go—seemingly small things like a barking dog or an abandoned vehicle or constant jaywalking—it leads to real and more visible decline."

San Franciscans went into shock in November 1978 when Mayor George Moscone and Supervisor Milk were assassinated by former San Francisco police officer and supervisor Dan White. White had been elected to the Board of Supervisors to represent a blue-collar, primarily white district. He did not grasp the necessity of compromising with those who represented San Francisco's other, more diverse districts, and he and Milk regularly clashed, with the politically astute Milk usually coming out the winner. These frustrations, along with the difficulty of surviving on what was then less than a $10,000 annual supervisor salary, led White to resign. This did not please White's constituents—many of whom were also his friends and neighbors—and in an attempt to save face White went to Mayor Moscone and asked to be reappointed to the now vacant position. White was sure he would be given back his job but Moscone, heavily lobbied by Milk, decided to give the supervisor's seat to someone else. White was furious, and took his revenge. He snuck into city hall, past the metal detectors, went to Moscone's office and shot him dead, then proceeded down the hall to Harvey Milk and killed him as well.

Hurley also knew White (they had played softball together) and says one of the truly unfortunate things was that if you looked at their voting records, White and Milk weren't that far apart. "Their problem was their cultural differences. And Dan had no idea how to play politics. He took it all personally." Hurley dealt with the results of White's inability to handle political and personal pressures as part of the tactical team called in to monitor the spontaneous vigil that erupted after the assassinations. Though the postassassination vigil was peaceful, the reaction to the result of White's trial was not. He received a seven-year sentence for the two murders because the defense successfully claimed "diminished capacity" (temporary insanity, supposedly due in part to excessive consumption of Hostess Twinkies), which resulted in a riot at city hall. "When civic crises erupt, officers from every division are called in. No matter what the officers' regular positions—animal control, robbery detail—they are trained and prepared for just such special tactical operations."

▓ TYPICAL DUTIES OF UNIFORMED OFFICERS

Both Hurley and Lark believe that an officer's ability to deal effectively with any situation, be it civic unrest or a traffic stop, results from experience both on the street and working with the community. Both are great promoters of volunteering, and both note a disturbing trend that many new hires show little interest in doing so. Lark attributes some of it to the fact that there simply aren't enough older officers in his department to mentor younger cops and bring them into the fold. "In our department of thirty-eight, half are new hires. I was able to spend a lot of time with older cops who didn't just teach me a lot but got me involved. New cops just don't have that." In San Francisco, the opportunity to earn extra income consumes the time officers used to give back to the community. "With overtime and off-duty work like security for all of the movies that are shot here, an officer can make $100,000 a year," Hurley says. "There used to be restrictions on overtime and extra duty, but not anymore. Sometimes these people work eighteen-hour days."

Something else that separates city officers from their small-town counterparts is the likelihood that they don't live in the town where they work. "I've lived in San Francisco all my life," Hurley says, "but now most of the officers live out in the suburbs an hour or more away. Their lives and their families just aren't a part of the city the way they were when I first got involved with the department."

One of the things that made Hurley such an asset to the force was a commitment to following up on every complaint received on his watch. This diligence had an unexpected payoff. Hurley met Jeannie Adamo while citing her for an incident in which her dog bit a neighbor. The dog was found not guilty by reason of self-defense, and as for Jeannie—well, a couple of years later Mark married her!

Whether in a big city or a small town, the range of an officer's duties is basically the same.

Basic Patrol Positions

Police officers are all sworn to "protect and serve," but they do it in a variety of ways:

Foot Patrol Officers

They have the most immediate contact with citizens. Walking the beat means being on a first-name basis with shop owners, community leaders and activists, and neighborhood residents. This can be a real asset when crimes occur. It is easier for officers to identify and capture the suspect, secure the crime scene, and interview witnesses when they know the area and have earned people's trust.

Car Patrol Officers

They have the same responsibility to patrol neighborhoods and respond to and secure crime scenes as their pedestrian counterparts. They also enforce traffic laws.

Motorcycle Patrol Officers

They are assigned primarily to traffic control and enforcement. Motorcycles allow officers far greater speed and agility than do patrol cars.

Horse Patrol Officers

They cover areas inaccessible to cars and motorcycles. Particularly effective in large crowds such as sporting events and concerts, the raised vantage point from the horse enables the officer to easily spot trouble and reach it quickly.

Bicycle Patrol Officers

They are assigned primarily in congested and confined areas, such as downtown locations, or crowded tourist destinations like Los Angeles's Venice Beach promenade. The ability to weave through crowds, alleys, and busy streets makes bicycle patrols particularly effective in narcotics enforcement.

Hurley describes how patrol styles differ from city to city: "I didn't need to pull people over for drunk driving because I'd patrol the bars on my beat and stop the customers before they got to their cars. I'd take them back into the bar, inform the bartender that they'd overserved the patron and that they needed to get them safely home. If I saw someone in a bad way and wasn't sure where they'd come from, I'd take them home myself. In some cities I think the officers are much more likely to see a person who's had too much to drink, let them get into their car and drive a few blocks, and then pull them over and arrest them. I never got that. Better just to keep the problem from happening in the first place. That way you get a reputation in the neighborhood as a good, fair cop, and the people will work with you to help keep trouble from happening."

Special Patrol Positions

Some uniformed officer positions require additional training, and may also require the officer to serve a specific number of years on the force before being considered for that position.

SWAT (Special Weapons and Tactics) Officers

They are trained in special weapons and tactics, sharpshooting, and hostage negotiations. They are generally required to have a minimum of five years of experience as a police officer before being considered for the unit.

The California Association of Tactical Officers (CATO)

They offer this sampling on their Web site (www.cactive.com/cato) of some of the recent newsworthy efforts of SWAT teams around the country:

Dallas, Texas (August 1999). After a three-hour standoff, during which twenty-year-old Melvin Johnson held his girlfriend hostage while officers tried unsuccessfully to negotiate her release, SWAT officers entered the apartment. Finding Johnson with a gun to his girlfriend's head, police shot him, sending Johnson to the hospital but allowing his hostage to escape unharmed.

Austell, Georgia (July 1999). A neighborhood dispute ended in tragedy when Greg Smith, forty, argued with neighbors and shot a police officer who came to investigate. Smith then barricaded himself and his seventy-three-year-old mother in their home for more than fifteen hours as a SWAT team surrounded the house. Afraid for the elderly woman's safety, SWAT officers entered the home and two were killed in the process. Smith was subsequently shot and killed by a SWAT sniper.

La Plata County, Colorado (July 13, 1999). An armed and suicidal man who eluded SWAT officers for two hours on horseback was captured with only minor injury when a

SWAT-team member fired beanbag bullets at the man, knocking him from his horse and enabling officers to retrieve his loaded gun. (The beanbags are a nonlethal means of stopping a suspect; they have been available since 1990.)

Air Patrol Officers

They use aircraft, generally helicopters, to track suspects fleeing in cars or on foot. They also patrol wilderness areas, assist during riots and with SWAT actions, and aid in search-and-rescue missions. Officers who wish to join this unit must be trained pilots with a Federal Aviation Administration (FAA) commercial-rated license.

K-9 Units

These consist of teamed human and canine crime fighters. Police officers generally need three years of service before being eligible for this unit. Highly trained tracking dogs with keen senses of smell are paired with policemen to search out suspects, bombs, and narcotics faster and more efficiently. The dogs are also trained to protect their human partners. Officer–canine initial training takes six weeks, but continues even after they become an official team. The officer–canine bond is a strong one; the dog usually lives with the officer and family.

■ APPLYING FOR AN OFFICER TRAINING PROGRAM

The process that determines whether or not an individual is chosen for an officer-training program is a lengthy one. The process is designed to separate those genuinely interested in a law enforcement career from those who aren't.

First, the applicant must fill out an application, complete a standard civil-service test, and pass a medical physical. For help in preparing for the civil-service test, which is a general knowledge exam, SAT and GED guides are useful, as are more specific study guides published by Barrons and Arco. According to Police Chief James Montgomery, approximately 12 percent of local police departments require officers to have some level of college education. Colleges and junior colleges offer majors in police science, law enforcement, and criminal justice.

Applicants who pass these initial tests move on to the second step. An oral interview is generally conducted by a panel of representatives from the police department and the personnel division. Questions cover the candidate's personal history, work history, education, and character. According to Jeff Geoghagan, a police academy instructor for the Seattle Police Department, the oral interview allows the board to observe how the candidate handles pressure and to look for character traits, both positive and negative, that could impact their ability to handle the job. Geoghagan recommends that the candidate take full advantage of this opportunity to display their communication skills and general enthusiasm for becoming a police officer. "Communication is so vital to do what we do," Geoghagan says, "because the vast majority is listening, understanding, and trying to reason with people. When an officer testifies in court it is essential that he or she come across as knowledgeable and articulate."

Professor Lee Libby, director of criminal justice at Shoreline Community College, suggests other things the board may consider during the interview: the candidate's ability to work with the public, classes they may have taken to prepare for the job, knowledge of current police issues, volunteer experience, and participation as a civilian in police ride-alongs. According to

Libby, the applicant should always expect to be asked about their willingness to use force in difficult situations. "With the use-of-force questions, the board members are trying to determine that you're not too quick to use force, but that you won't back away if you need to either."

According to Geoghagan, the board is looking for the following essential characteristics:

- The ability to make sound judgments.
- Maturity.
- Good moral character.
- Respect for others.
- Compassion.
- Good oral and written communication skills.
- Respect for the law.

Should the board determine that the candidate possesses all of the necessary qualifications, the final step is a series of psychological and psychiatric tests, a drug screen, and a background check. Once these are successfully completed, the applicant is ready for the police academy.

Becoming a Uniformed Police Officer

Qualifications

The qualifications to become a uniformed police officer include:

- At least twenty-one years old.
- High-school diploma or its equivalent.
- Valid driver's license and good driving record.
- Pass a physical fitness test (minimum standards determined by the department).

- Vision correctable to 20/20.
- Pass an extensive written test.
- Pass an oral interview.
- Pass a polygraph examination.
- Submit to and pass a background check.

Salary and Benefits

Beginning salaries range widely for each jurisdiction. However, the average is between $29,000 and $42,000 annually, depending on the department's size and location. Officer benefit packages generally include medical and dental plans, life insurance, sick leave, annual vacation, and a retirement plan with the option to retire at age fifty-five or after twenty-five years of service, whichever comes first.

Putting Together the Pieces
Detectives

FROM THE CLASSIC SHERLOCK HOLMES TO THE GRIT OF TV'S *NYPD Blue*, perhaps no one profession provides more or better storytelling opportunities than that of the detective. Detectives face the darkest elements of humanity daily. They must rely upon their wits, experience, and intuition not only to find the criminal, but also to secure the evidence and build the case that will convict them.

■ THE DETECTIVE'S RANGE OF DUTIES

Dressed in plainclothes, the detective (known in some jurisdictions as "inspector") arrives at a crime scene prepared for anything: to interview witnesses, collect evidence, gather facts, interrogate suspects, examine pertinent records, conduct background checks and follow-up interviews, and possibly make arrests. Criminal cases are won or lost based on how effectively detectives do their jobs. Contaminated evidence, an improperly interrogated suspect, or a poorly executed search warrant can result in a criminal going free. It is the detective's job to make sure that doesn't happen.

The detective is almost never the first one on the scene, but is summoned after a patrol officer has made initial contact and cordoned off the crime site.

Detectives note every aspect of the crime, such as the location and position of the body or living victim (if one is involved) and every physical detail of the surroundings, for example an open window if the crime took place in a home, or trampled grass if the site is an open field. Detectives need to consider not only the witnesses on or near the scene but also where unknown witnesses might have been, and do whatever possible to track them down.

Once the crime scene has been properly contained and evidence collected, it is the detective's responsibility to create a log detailing each item of evidence, the time and date of its collection, and each and every person involved in that process. In the O.J. Simpson case, a delay in logging evidence (the defendant's blood sample) created an appearance of impropriety. Such mistakes may create a flaw or break in the chain of evidence from which the prosecution can not recover.

■ TYPICAL DIVISIONS WITHIN THE DETECTIVE'S BUREAU

Unless the department is an extremely small one, detectives are generally assigned to specific divisions. Although they have regularly assigned shifts, detectives are actually always on call and never know when they might be summoned to organize a new investigation or investigate new leads on a case already assigned to them.

Homicide

This elite squad of detectives is responsible for investigating deaths resulting or appearing to result from anything other than natural causes. The responsibilities of a homicide investigator are enormously difficult. In addition to their investigative duties, they are often called upon to notify the next of kin and escort them to the morgue for victim identification. Additionally, homicide detectives are frequently required to be present at the autopsy.

Sex Crimes

These detectives investigate rape and child sex abuse as well as "peeping Toms," cases of indecent exposure, and other sexually deviant behaviors. Detectives assigned to these units often receive special training in dealing effectively with profoundly traumatized victims. With the aid of trained physicians, detectives complete a "rape kit" when appropriate, collecting sperm, DNA, fiber, and other evidence from the victim. In recent years the dangers of stalking have also become clear. The murder of actress Rebecca Schaeffer resulted in the passage of California's stalking law, the first in the nation. The Los Angeles Police Department is proud of their "stalking unit," a group of detectives dedicated to stopping the pursuit and harassment of stalking victims, many of whom have been chosen nearly at random by their harasser.

Domestic Violence Unit

As knowledge and awareness of domestic battery becomes increasingly sophisticated, so do the detective units that investigate these crimes. Once dismissed as a private problem between husband and wife, domestic violence is now seen for what it is, a brutal crime that severely undermines the whole community as well as the families immediately involved. Now empowered to arrest offenders whether or not the spouse files a complaint, detectives do more than haul the perpetrator off to jail. They advise the abused person on options such as shelters and involve social services to ensure that children in violent homes get the assistance they need.

Vice Squad

Charged to investigate such crimes as prostitution, drug trafficking, and illegal gambling, vice detectives often work undercover and are assigned to some of the seediest and most dangerous areas.

Narcotics

Enforcers of the state's narcotics laws and statutes, these detectives often work undercover to arrange narcotics purchases and obtain information about major suppliers and distributors of illegal drugs. Drug-related forfeiture laws give officers broad power to seize items that may have been obtained with ill-gotten gains. These items are often sold later at auction, and the profits go back to the department. Because of the nationwide war on drugs, these officers are more likely to work regularly with other law enforcement agencies.

Fraud/Forgery Unit

These officers deal with con artists, forgers, repeat offenders of bad check passing, and others who make their money by deceiving others. Detectives track down and bring these criminals to justice, and are involved in returning as much of the swindled victim's assets as possible.

Burglary/Theft Unit

This unit investigates property crimes against individuals and businesses, major robberies, corporate theft, auto theft, and related criminal activities such as shops dedicated to disassembling and reselling parts from stolen cars. Detectives also investigate those trafficking in stolen goods, including known "fences," some pawnshops, and private gun dealers.

Gang Activities Unit

The proliferation of gangs gives this unit a special importance. A well-run gang activities unit can literally change the face of a neighborhood from one whose residents cower indoors to avoid gunfire to a place where children can play on the streets and businesses can prosper. These detectives use a variety of methods, such as tracking gang leaders and their affiliates, keeping tabs on newly paroled gang members, and reaching out to the community so that neighbors feel safe enough to testify against "gang-bangers."

Internal Affairs Division (IAD)

This division is responsible for protecting the public from cops who use their power to victimize rather than protect the public. IAD investigates a wide range of cases, from the brutal beating and sodomy attack against Abner Louima in New York City, to cops who use or sell the narcotics they confiscate, to the local beat cop who considers free lunch at restaurants on his patrol to be a job entitlement. IAD officers are alerted to problems within the department by citizen complaints. They also monitor officers with repeated behavior problems, investigate drug or property theft in police stations, and follow up on complaints by fellow officers.

Computer Crimes

These specialists cover a range of crimes, using their skills to track on-line pedophiles one day, to secret-stealing hackers the next. As the use of computers grows, so does the perpetration of computer crimes, making this one of the fastest growing areas of law enforcement.

Becoming a Police Detective

To become a police detective one must have successfully met all job requirements for a uniformed officer and completed academy training.

Qualifications

Job qualifications for police detectives include:

- Served a minimum of four to five years as a uniformed officer.
- Pass written proficiency tests.
- Participate in an oral interview conducted by a panel of superior officers.

Salary

Detective salaries range from $38,000 to $44,000 annually.

CHAPTER THREE

County and Statewide Protectors
The Sheriff's Department and the State Police

BETWEEN THE SMALL-TOWN POLICE STATIONS AND BIG-CITY police departments lie acres of rural counties, miles of unincorporated roads, and hundreds of little towns unable to support a police force of their own. When crime occurs here, outside the jurisdiction of local police departments, it falls to either the county sheriff's department or the state police (also known as state troopers) to bring the perpetrators to justice.

■ THE SHERIFF'S DEPARTMENT

Say "sheriff" and most people think of the craggy-faced fellow standing between lawless bandits and a small Western town, or the pot-bellied redneck extorting exorbitant traffic fines on secluded country roads. The truth is that the sheriff's department is a complex, hi-tech law enforcement agency that is as likely to be tracking computer criminals in cyberspace as pulling reluctant motorists over for traffic violations.

The department is staffed by deputy sheriffs and headed by the sheriff, an elected official who generally serves four-year terms. Sheriffs have the same authority and perform many of the same duties as their metropolitan police counterparts and in rural areas are often the primary law-enforcement agency.

Duties Exclusive to the Sheriff's Department

While sheriffs' departments have many of the same duties as the local police, they differ in some vital ways.

Civil Process Procedures

Deputy sheriffs are responsible for carrying out civil-process-related procedures such as serving subpoenas and eviction notices, seizing property, and working in conjunction with the police where appropriate.

Presiding over County Jails

In many areas the sheriff's department is responsible for jail oversight. They are in charge of the county jail and its occupants twenty-four hours a day, transporting them from jail to the courthouse, other jurisdictions, or the hospital. Jailhouse provisions and maintenance are also the sheriff's responsibility.

Court Security

The sheriff's department is in charge of providing security for the courthouse. Court security is a presence in each courtroom to guard against violence by any participant in the proceedings. Deputies are also stationed at courthouse entrances to operate X ray machines and metal detectors and prevent weapons from being brought into the building. Courthouse security officers may be sworn sheriff's deputies or contracted private security, but the sheriff's department is the final authority over anyone working in court security.

Asset Investigation

The right to seize assets enables the sheriff's department to run the narcotics asset seizure unit, which is responsible for investigating the money trail from illegal drugs. Drug laws and money-laundering statutes allow deputies to seize the illegal proceeds of drug activity. Local police may take physical possession of property, but it falls solely to the sheriff's deputies to serve papers and post notices of seizure when appropriate.

Sex Offender Registration Program

Sex offenders must now be registered with local authorities and their identities and whereabouts are made available to the public through a computer database. In conjunction with this program, any person seeking to work with children in a county- or state-sponsored job or activity—ranging from schoolteacher to volunteer soccer coach—must be fingerprinted and pass a background check. Municipal police departments and sheriffs' offices keep such databases, but in smaller municipalities the primary registration is through the sheriff's office.

Major Accident Response and Reconstruction (MARR)

This unit investigates fatality and serious-injury accidents. Officers in this unit receive specialized training including basic accident investigation, computer diagramming, photography, and accident site and advanced traffic reconstruction. Although municipal officers also handle accident scenes, the size and scope of the sheriff department's jurisdiction involves them in many more reconstruction activities and contributes to their expertise in this area.

Automated Fingerprint Identification Service (AFIS)

This unit, staffed by nonsworn personnel, maintains the sheriff's fingerprint identification database, statistics, and sex-offender registrations. AFIS provides identification services for immigration officials, the medical examiner's office, and other police agencies.

Field Operations

These units provide law enforcement to cities that cannot afford their own police force as well as in unincorporated areas. These cities contract for services with the sheriff's department. Officers are trained to accommodate each area's specific needs. This unit is also responsible for training new recruits.

Duties Shared with Police Departments

The sheriff's department has divisions that mirror those of a municipal police department. Sheriffs' deputies work patrol and traffic, narcotics and drug enforcement, major investigations (including homicide, felony assault, and missing children), domestic violence, and sexual assaults.

Criminal Investigations

Major Fabienne Brooks, head of the King County Sheriff's Department's criminal investigation unit, is the highest-ranked African-American female officer in the state of Washington.

She comes from a long line of law enforcement. Her father was a military man, and her uncle was the first black officer to attend the FBI National Academy. After graduating from college, she worked as an investigator for the public defender's office but felt frustrated by the process. "I kept seeing lawyers, who were doing their jobs of course, getting people off and I thought maybe I was working for the wrong side."

In 1978, Brooks became the first African-American woman hired by the sheriff's office of King County. She's since moved up through the ranks with extraordinary success, working homicide, sexual assault, and finally being assigned precinct commander. For Brooks, some assignments stand out. "We were responsible for initiating the implementation of the registered sexual offender program and for the development of the domestic violence intervention unit, which focuses on improving the handling of domestic violence cases." Brooks also experienced firsthand the frustrations of police work when she was assigned as a follow-up homicide investigator on the notorious Green River case, in which a serial killer took the lives of forty-nine women between 1984 and 1988. There were problems dealing with the media, for example. "The challenge was to give enough information to the media without compromising the investigation. We didn't want to give out information that only the killer would know because, believe it or not, we had people coming in and confessing to being the killer," Brooks says. The ultimate frustration, though, was that the killer was never found. "I'm still haunted by the fact that the case was never officially solved. Even now when I read the papers and a case seems similar, it's in the back of my mind that he (the killer) has moved on to a different area." To let go of these difficult cases, Brooks believes it's vital that an officer has some life experience so that they can gain perspective and move on. "You can't do this job for the money," Brooks says. "You have to do it because you really want to."

Community Relations

Like the local police, the sheriff's department maintains a community policing division, which works on outreach and better officer-citizen relations. Sheriff David Reichert has been a member of Washington State's King County Sheriff's Department for nearly thirty years. King County, located in western Washington, is the largest county in the state of Washington and includes the city of Seattle. For Reichert, the department's key goal is providing quality professional law enforcement services tailored for individual communities.

"We directly serve more than 600,000 people," Reichert says. "My focus is to move toward more prevention in law enforcement. As a matter of fact, we realized that our officers needed more training in problem-solving so one of the changes we made was to increase the hours of training in that area." To that end, Reichert has established "storefronts." An example of community policing, storefronts are placed in strategic locations within communities, allowing citizens easier access and the ability to interact with law enforcement officers. In 1997, citizen academies were established with the goal of informing and educating local government, business, and neighborhood leaders about the services of the sheriff's office. "Once you build a relationship with people," Reichert says, "you build trust."

Reichert has also focused units on particular areas where he feels the department can make a difference. One is the family support unit. "We have more than 70,000 warrants issued for parents who aren't paying their child support. It's also an intervention method because once the financial support starts, people become emotionally involved with their children again." Reichert believes these actions today will have lasting advantages. "Down the road I think we're going to see the benefits. Not as many kids are going to be in the system."

Reichert was injured during a domestic violence call early in his career, and it left a lasting impression that such cases are dangerous not only for the victims but for responding officers as well. This formed his desire to stop domestic violence early on, before it gets out of control. "Our domestic violence unit tries to focus on the misdemeanors and offer intervention before it graduates to physical violence. We want to better serve our community and do more than just respond to a call and drive away. We want to handle the situation for the long term."

Reichert believes that part of being effective is to form partnerships with all branches of law enforcement. "If I arrest someone for brandishing a gun, and the people at the courts say no dice, we're full, then my purpose is defeated. Therefore it's my job to get everyone on board."

Becoming a Deputy Sheriff

What does Reichert think has changed since he joined the force? "When I was hired they were looking for people with buffed physiques. Now, slowly, over the years, you see people who are more service-oriented, people who want to work with and improve the quality of life in the community. Those are the characteristics I look for in new officers."

Chief Brooks feels the same way, and stresses to potential officers the necessary qualities that any law enforcement officer should have: integrity, honesty, and leadership ability. "It's very important to uphold these qualities. Everyone makes mistakes, but careless disregard can smear a whole department and policing in general. Just look at some of the reactions to and generalizations aimed at police officers as a result of some of the current events in the news that negatively involve police officers." Brooks also believes community policing can help combat these negative impressions. "With community policing programs, citizens are more cooperative and my officers have an easier time in neighborhoods. People want to know the truth about crime rates and burglaries, speeding and traffic problems, and what we as the police are going to do about them. Communicate your responses accurately and effectively and you retain the community's confidence and respect."

Qualifications

Although there may be some variance by municipality, the basic qualifications for the position of deputy sheriff include:

- At least twenty-one years old.
- High-school diploma or its equivalent.
- Pass a written (civil service) test.
- Pass a physical fitness test, minimum standards determined by the department.
- Valid driver's license and good driving record.
- Vision correctable to 20/20.
- Pass a background investigation that includes a polygraph examination, psychological testing, and a medical examination.

Salary

The beginning salaries for sheriffs' deputies range from $29,800 to $36,500 annually.

■ STATE TROOPERS

Whether under the moniker of trooper, police, or highway patrol, these officers work concurrently with other law enforcement officers in varied ways such as aiding in criminal investigations or helping stranded motorists on the highway. State police do the majority of their work on the nation's highways, enforcing traffic and safety laws, directing accident-scene traffic, administering first aid, calling for emergency vehicles, and reconstructing and determining an accident's cause.

To get an idea of the magnitude of the trooper's job, consider these 1998 statistics for the Ohio state troopers. In that year alone, Ohio's troopers assisted more then 500,000 motorists, investigated nearly 80,000 crashes, and made 850,000 traffic arrests (including 24,667 for driving under the influence and more than 192,000 for safety-belt and child-safety-restraint violations). Additionally, Ohio state troopers issued 440,000 warnings in 1998.

Troopers also provide aid in a variety of civic situations. In the event of disaster, troopers keep the public informed of weather conditions and road closures, secure disaster areas, and patrol hazardous roadways to keep the public out. They supplement the efforts of local law enforcement, who may be overwhelmed when nature creates havoc. Troopers also provide aid during more upbeat civic events, such as escorting VIPs and dignitaries to public functions. Additionally, state troopers are involved in the investigation of criminal activity that takes place on state-owned property.

Becoming a State Trooper

Chief Annette Sandberg, head of the Washington state patrol unit, describes a real difference between working as a state trooper and other law enforcement jobs. Patrolling the highways requires troopers to work alone most of the time. "What I look for in a state patrol officer is someone who is self-motivated, can work unsupervised, is proactive, and of course who is honest and has integrity, first and foremost. Troopers come in contact with the public a great deal so they must be courteous yet authoritative, and have the ability to think quickly on their feet."

State troopers aren't just concerned with getting bad drivers off the road. They're also very involved in educating the public to prevent dangerous traffic situations. Troopers visit schools to educate children about the dangers of speeding and drunk driving. They also share this message with community groups and offer classes and seminars for interested adults. When it comes to public safety, the state trooper is there to both protect and prevent.

Qualifications

Although there may be some variance by jurisdiction, in general the qualifications for state police officers include:

- Between twenty-one and thirty years old.
- U.S. citizen.
- Good driving record.
- No felony arrests.
- High-school diploma or its equivalent (a two- or four-year degree is desirable for advancement).
- Good physical condition.
- Pass written and oral exams.
- Submit to and pass drug tests.

Salary

Starting salaries for state troopers range from $29,000 to $35,700 annually, depending upon the size and location of the department.

CHAPTER FOUR

Keeping a Nation Safe
The FBI

G IVEN THE STATUS AND RESPECT AFFORDED TODAY'S FEDERAL
Bureau of Investigation (FBI), it's difficult to imagine
that its earliest incarnation in 1908 was as a minor one.
Originally an unnamed force of special agents (appointed by
then–Attorney General Charles J. Bonaparte under President
Theodore Roosevelt), the squad was created to relieve the
Secret Service of lesser federal investigations such as bank-
ruptcy fraud and neutrality and antitrust violations. It took
two legislative actions designed to inhibit vice, and a man
whose mission in life was to catalogue the vices of others,
J. Edgar Hoover, to bring what we now know as the FBI to the
prominence it holds today. The Mann Act of 1910 made it
illegal to transport women across state lines for "immoral
purposes," while ratification of the Eighteenth Amendment
made alcohol illegal (popularly known as Prohibition).

■ THE RISE OF THE MODERN-DAY FBI

America was a mass of contradictions in the 1920s. Wild Jazz
Age youth flouted the temperance-obsessed promoters of
Prohibition; money flowed on Wall Street while hard times

hit rural areas, promoting racism and the Ku Klux Klan; and citizens who would never before have broken the law were selling liquor to gangsters. In the midst of this chaos, the then-titled Bureau of Investigation flourished. Public outrage over the expansion of organized crime (which, ironically, was funded largely by the monies made violating Prohibition) resulted in the agency's 1934 empowerment to do more than investigate; agents could now carry guns and make arrests. In 1935, Hoover was promoted from assistant to director of the FBI, a post he held until his death in 1972.

Hoover, who began his government career in the Library of Congress, used his lifelong love of keeping files on others (a habit he started while keeping diaries as a youth) as a ladder to the top. After a transfer to the job of file clerk in the Justice Department, Hoover was the focus of much attention for two reasons: he was one of the few young and vital men in Washington, D.C. (most were serving in World War I), and he possessed extraordinary attention to detail combined with an immaculate appearance. He caught the eye of fervent antiradical Attorney General A. Mitchell Palmer, who put him in charge of the General Intelligence Division, an agency charged with seeking out communists. Palmer's successor, Harry Daugherty, was happy to discover that Hoover was as good at keeping records on the attorney general's political enemies as he was on anarchists. So Hoover's rise continued, unabated, until he took over as director of the Bureau of Investigation (the name was changed to the Federal Bureau of Investigation in 1935) under President Coolidge.

Hoover's tenure started with a clean sweep of the remainders of the corrupt Harding administration. He fired dozens of agents and established standards for spit-and-polish appearance and by-the-book law enforcement that remain to this day. Over the decades the agency has grown in scope as an investigator of espionage, sedition, and draft violations during wartime; a watchdog of the Black Panthers of the 1960s and the white supremacists of today; and a monitor of civil rights leaders like Martin Luther King, Jr. In addition to this, the FBI plays a prominent role as the last, and some might say best, line of defense against the worst kind of felons, serial killers, kidnappers, pedophilia rings, and violent criminals who cross the country leaving destruction behind them.

Public scrutiny and revelations of Hoover's secret files have made today's FBI a less autonomous and better-reviewed agency than it was under his reign. Still, the agency is not without its detractors. Questions remain about how hundreds of FBI files were transferred into the hands of the then-new Clinton administration's inexperienced head of security. FBI Chief Louis Freeh found himself the subject of some controversy for his outspoken public support of independent counsel Kenneth Starr.

In most organizations, those in charge deal with politics, and the FBI is no exception. And like most agencies, it is the long-term and often unsung people running the day-to-day functions that make the FBI the effective crime-fighting force it is today.

FBI DIVISIONS AND JURISDICTIONS

There are numerous investigative units within the FBI. Most of their cases are long-term and highly complex, often worked with task forces involving federal, state, local, and foreign law enforcement agencies. Whether working alone or with other agencies, the FBI divides its investigations into several major programs.

The FBI's jurisdiction over a crime is determined by several factors, including where the crime took place; if the crime violates federal law; or if the crime involves the crossing of state lines, such as with interstate kidnapping or car theft.

Major Crimes and Major Offenders

This program is responsible for investigating a broad range of criminal activities, including:

- The assault, kidnapping, or killing of the president, vice president, or member of Congress.
- Kidnapping and extortion.
- The sexual exploitation of children.
- Bank robbery, burglary, or robbery.
- Crime on Native American reservations.
- Crime aboard aircraft.
- Tampering with consumer products.
- Theft from interstate shipments.
- Interstate transport of stolen motor vehicles and other property.
- Theft of federal government property.
- Unlawful flight across state lines to avoid prosecution (including fugitives related to parental kidnapping).

Counterterrorism

This division is responsible for the investigation of domestic terrorism (such as the Oklahoma City bombing), hostage-taking, nuclear extortion, murder or attempted murder of American citizens abroad, and bombings or attempted bombings.

Currently this unit is part of the multijurisdictional effort seeking Eric Robert Rudolph, who in 1998 was charged with bombing the New Woman All Women Health Care Clinic in

Birmingham, Alabama. Targeted as an abortion provider, the clinic bombing took the life of a Birmingham police officer and seriously injured a head nurse. Not long after his indictment, Rudolph disappeared into the Nantahala forest in western North Carolina. Aided by his excellent survival skills, and the antigovernment and antiabortion sentiments of many of the area's residents, Rudolph still eludes capture. Since his original indictment Rudolph has been linked to several Atlanta-area bombings, including the Centennial Park blast that took a life during the 1996 Summer Olympics.

Organized Crime and Drug

This program empowers agents to investigate drug trafficking, and other elements of organized crime such as money laundering, criminal enterprise, and labor racketeering. The Racketeer Influenced and Corrupt Organization (RICO) statute has been a remarkably effective weapon in the war on organized crime.

The broad investigative powers offered by RICO allow the agents greater leeway when it comes to wiretapping, a major factor in bringing down Mafia bosses such as John Gotti. The case against Gotti was built on conversations recorded by devices placed in his favorite hangouts. Gotti was heard discussing his involvement in loan sharking, corruption of labor unions, assault, and murder. He also had some harsh words for his then right-hand man Sammy "The Bull" Gravano. When FBI agents approached Gravano with evidence of his boss's disfavor, Gravano turned and gave testimony that, among other felonies, Gotti had ordered the execution of boss Paul Castellano. Based on this testimony, Gotti was put away for life in 1992.

National Computer Crime Squad (NCSS)

Noted for its expertise in combating computer crime, the squad is responsible for investigating unauthorized entry into major computer networks in both the private and government sectors.

Investigations include major computer network intrusions, industrial espionage, pirating of computer software, and intrusions into government, financial, medical, and federal-interest computers. The NCSS also investigates illegal cable- and satellite-signal interceptions and copyright laws as they relate to computer software.

Civil Rights

This division involves agents in the investigation of crimes based on race, gender, or sexual orientation. These range from housing and credit discrimination to headline-grabbing acts of violence such as the bombing of African-American churches, "hate crimes" such as the race-based murder of Jewish radio-talk-show host Alan Berg, and complaints of excessive force or property damage by police officers.

Foreign Counterintelligence

This division is responsible for detecting, maintaining intelligence, and countering the actions of foreign intelligence organizations that are engaged in espionage and information-gathering adversely affecting the United States.

Financial Crime

These agents investigate the corruption of public officials and election law violations, fraud against the government, health-care fraud, bank fraud and embezzlement, and environmental crime.

Applicant Matters

This department conducts background checks on those applying for positions within sensitive government agencies. Those positions include:

- White House staff.
- U.S. court candidates.
- Staff of the Justice and Energy departments.
- FBI agent and FBI support personnel.

Behavioral Sciences

While not one of the major crimes division, the Behavioral Science Unit has gained great notoriety due to its portrayal in films and television. The unit gained credibility by offering major assistance in some notorious cases of the 1970s, and the number of agents assigned to this work multiplied from a handful to dozens today.

Data Clearinghouses

Two vital data banks aid the FBI and other agencies in pursuing criminals and assessing crime trends throughout the nation.

Uniform Crime Reporting

This division collects crime statistics on serious offenses throughout the nation. More than 16,000 U.S. law enforcement agencies submit data to this system, which is used by the FBI to predict and plot crime trends.

The National Crime Information Center (NCIC)

This information center is available to all law enforcement officers twenty-four hours a day. It provides constant access to information on crimes such as murder, wanted or missing persons, and stolen property. It also contains extensive history on known criminals, including arrest records and "modus operandi," the personal signatures left by the criminal at each of the crime scenes. (For example, a burglar might always help himself to a meal after his break-ins, or a rapist might restrain each of his victims in the same way.)

■ INTERNAL ORGANIZATION OF THE FBI

The FBI headquarters in Washington, D.C. has nine divisions, each of which is headed by an assistant director. These are subdivided into offices, headed by an inspector or general counsel and supported by deputies, section chiefs, unit chiefs, and supervisors. Together they oversee fifty-six field offices, more than 400 satellite offices (known as resident agencies), four specialized field installations, and twenty-three foreign posts called legal attachés.

Field offices are headed by a special agent in charge (SAC), who has one or more assistant SACs (depending on the size of the office). They in turn manage squads of special agents and are supported by an office services manager. The resident agencies are managed by resident agents who must report to the SAC in charge of their territory, who then reports to the director's office. Legal attachés report to the criminal investigation division.

Support Positions within the FBI

Below are a variety of civilian positions that are available within the FBI, and are largely representative of all federal law enforcement agencies.

- Professional, such as attorney, accountant, chemist, civil engineer, and contract specialist.
- Administration, such as budget analyst, accounting technician, telecommunications, writer/editor, purchasing agent, administrative assistant, and clerical support.
- Technical, such as computer programmer, systems specialist, operations support, and language specialist.

For a complete listing of these and other positions available within federal law enforcement, contact the FBI's central office or a local field office (see appendix).

Becoming an FBI Agent

FBI agents come from a variety of backgrounds. Marita Malone, currently a supervising agent for the FBI, started her working career as an English teacher and track and basketball coach. A bureau agent for sixteen years, Malone also has a Ph.D. in public administration. "I'm a service-oriented person, like people who work in government," Malone says. "I was burned-out on teaching so I applied for what I thought was the best job in public service, and that was with the FBI. FBI agents are representatives of the public and it's a job that we take seriously. The qualities that we uphold are fidelity to the right things, bravery for the right things, and integrity in all things."

Malone enthusiastically recommends the FBI as a career with limitless opportunities and work that is important and interesting, particularly for women. "Before Hoover died in 1972, a handful of women were employed as agents, usually in clerical jobs, and another handful were in the applicant stages. After Hoover's death, the door was opened to all qualified women." As a supervisor, Malone's role is much different than during her days as a special agent. "Special agents are out investigating cases, talking to people, developing leads. As a supervisor, I work out problems. I have resident agencies, and a lot of my time is spent trying to get them the resources they need. It's not unusual for me to be at the office at six-thirty in the morning and leave at seven at night. All you need is one big case to tie up your resources and your life."

Qualifications

As the primary investigative law enforcement agency of the Department of Justice, FBI requirements are among the most restrictive in law enforcement. The qualifications to become an FBI agent include:

- U.S. citizenship.
- Between the ages of twenty-three and thirty-seven at the time of appointment.
- Bachelor's degree from an accredited college or university.
- Pass a drug test (applicants are disqualified for use of marijuana within the previous three years or any other drug in the previous ten years).
- Agree to and pass a polygraph examination.
- Pass a color vision test.
- Valid driver's license and good driving record.
- Pass a credit check.
- Pass a complete background check and supply personal references.

- Pass an oral interview.
- Three years of full-time work experience.

Newly hired agents and support personnel are required to be available to relocate to any of the FBI field offices during the first ten years of service. After that, relocation is voluntary.

Certain hiring requirements may be waived if the FBI applicant has specialized skills. For example, since agents are required to understand and interpret complex laws and statutes, a law degree is a desirable asset that could result in the waiver of some criteria. An accounting degree is valuable when it comes to duties such as tracing, analyzing, and interpreting the intricacies of financial and accounting records. Foreign-language proficiency along with a college degree in any field may also be a special qualifying factor.

For those interested in working with NCCS (the computer crime division), additional job requirements include:

- Degree in computer science.
- Prior work in the computer industry or an academic institution.
- Basic and advanced computer training.
- Experience with UNIX and other computer operating systems.
- Knowledge of basic data and telecommunications networks.

Salary and Benefits

Starting salaries for FBI agents range from $36,500 to $40,000 annually. Typical for all federal officers, benefits generally include a comprehensive retirement program through the Federal Employee Retirement System, low-cost insurance, paid federal holidays, and annual leave earned at a rate of thirteen days per year.

The Founding Fathers
of Law Enforcement
U.S. Marshals

A PROMINENT DOCTOR IS CONVICTED OF MURDER. DURING THE bus ride, which is to take the doctor to prison for life, another convict attacks a guard and engineers an escape. The doctor escapes as well, and so begins a manhunt to which massive resources of money, time, and manpower are committed until the fugitive is returned to justice. This particular scenario is a fiction—as fans of the hit film *The Fugitive* surely recognize—but its depiction of a U.S. marshal action is, according to the agency members interviewed for this book, extraordinarily accurate. It is also the basis for whatever knowledge most of us have of the workings of the U.S. Marshal Service—the oldest law enforcement agency in the United States.

President George Washington established the U.S. Marshals in 1789. Although the deputies were given extensive authority to support the laws and the courts, their initial duties were limited mainly to the Washington, D.C. area where they served writs, warrants, subpoenas, and summonses, made arrests, and handled prisoners. Washington soon realized that a more expansive police agency was needed, one that could enforce laws and carry them out uniformly throughout the country as well as represent the federal government in local territories, many of which had no law enforcement of their own. Marshals began to travel the nation collecting statistical information, and took the national census in 1879.

■ DUTIES OF THE MARSHALS SERVICE

The agency was also involved in some of the less illustrious moments of our nation's history; they worked as trackers to capture fugitive slaves and later were responsible for the registration of so-called "enemy aliens" such as Americans of Japanese descent who were interned during World War II. Fortunately, such duties are no longer a part of the Marshals Service, which now spends its resources protecting all U.S. citizens.

Fugitive Investigations

As shown in *The Fugitive,* the U.S. Marshals Service has the primary authority to investigate when federal prisoners escape (except for FBI fugitives). Marshals are considered the best fugitive hunters in law enforcement; they truly won't rest until they get their suspect.

Such was the case when marshals went after Alphonse "Ollie Boy" Persico. The former head of a New York organized-crime family, Persico was convicted of loan sharking and faced up to sixty years in prison when he failed to show up for his 1980 sentencing hearing. It took seven years of following up on tips, canvassing neighborhoods, and tracking Persico's aliases, but in 1987 Persico was discovered at his hideout in a Connecticut apartment building and brought to justice. Thus continued the tradition that made the marshals the stuff of Old West legend with their relentless pursuits of Billy the Kid, Belle Starr, and Butch Cassidy and the Sundance Kid.

Deputy Marshal Dennis Behrend says variety makes the job fascinating: "You may track down the person who writes bad checks one day and track down an ax-murderer who escaped from federal custody the next."

Behrend was involved in tracking fugitive Christopher Boyce, a convicted spy who sold secret satellite information to the Soviets. The story of Boyce and his cocaine-addicted partner, Daulton Lee, was compellingly told in the book and subsequent film *The Falcon and the Snowman*. Both Lee and Boyce were serving forty-year sentences in 1980 when Boyce escaped confinement. "We had just assumed a great deal of fugitive capture authority in 1978 from the FBI so we wanted to prove ourselves," Behrend says. "It became one of our most important cases."

Behrend and his fellow deputies interviewed more than 800 people in the United States and abroad, eventually tracking the fugitive across the northwest United States. Boyce, meanwhile, had added to his criminal résumé by becoming a bank robber. Eventually the marshals narrowed down Boyce's location to Port Angeles, Washington, where they spent weeks undercover working in grocery and convenience stores and frequenting places popular with criminals. "It was a very difficult capture because Boyce simply started a new life. He completely cut off contact with people he knew so there was very little to go on," says Behrend, who spotted Boyce at a hamburger drive-in and, with his partner, arrested the fugitive quickly without incident. "That capture really put us over the top. Once we proved we could catch a national fugitive like Boyce, we gained a lot of credibility with other law enforcement agencies."

Behrend credits much of the marshals' success to the element of surprise. "We can wait for days, weeks, or months, when other law enforcement agencies may not be able to take that kind of time."

Since 1983, the Marshals Service has compiled its own "Fifteen Most Wanted" list of the most dangerous and notorious fugitives from justice. As captors of 55 percent of all federal fugitives, the marshals carry out more arrests than all other federal law enforcement agencies combined. Marshals also work with other agencies, lending their expertise and financial resources to aid in the capture of criminals at the state and local level. What began as an experiment has turned into a permanent and successful joint operation in more than 150 communities across the country.

Deputy Behrend notes, "A lot of times our job begins where another agency's responsibility has ended. For example, if the DEA (Drug Enforcement Agency) makes a drug bust, and that prisoner escapes, they are through with the case and we coordinate the capture."

Deputy marshals capture more than 19,000 fugitives a year, sponsor more than seventy-five federal task forces, and are responsible for 90 percent of wanted foreign fugitives living in the United States. The service has Interpol representatives in both Washington, D.C. and Lyon, France and is responsible for the tricky business of foreign extradition. Sometimes marshals must wait in another country for weeks monitoring a fugitive while extradition details are negotiated.

Behrend details the problems of extradition. "We have no authority to make arrests in foreign countries so we have to preplan and work with the local constabulary and they usually assign someone to work with us. My philosophy is following the six Ps. That's 'Proper Prior Planning Prevents Pathetic Performance.'"

The Witness Protection Program

When hit man and Los Angeles crime-family boss Jimmy "The Weasel" Fratiano was finally arrested, he had two options: life in prison or the probable death sentence that comes with being a "rat." "The Weasel" chose to take his chances with the mob and turned informer with the help of the Witness Section Program (WITSEC), more popularly known as the Witness Protection Program.

While some question the wisdom of putting a confessed murderer back into the general population, the Witness Section Program is lauded as a valuable tool in fighting crime. Witness testimony is a primary reason that law enforcement enjoys an 89 percent conviction rate. Moreover, less than 19 percent of those enrolled in the program return to a life of crime, a recidivism rate far lower than that of the general prison population.

Once the attorney general's office has determined that a witness is qualified for the program, the marshals brief potential participants on the rules of life within WITSEC. If these rules are agreed upon, the witness and family are relocated to a safe area, complete with documentation (such as new social security numbers and school records). In their new location, the family is provided with housing, medical care, a stipend for basic living expenses, job training, and employment until they become self-sufficient. Those in the program are afforded twenty-four-hour-a-day protection until they're safely settled in their new lives, and marshals later ensure their safety when they are brought back to the original jurisdiction to testify.

Protecting the Courts

Not only witnesses need protection. In recent years threats in the courthouse have increased significantly. As a result, the marshals also provide personal protection for federal judges, court officials, and jurors.

In more than 800 locations where court proceedings are held, marshal service court security officers detected more than 350,000 weapons in 1998. On average approximately 300 threats against court officials are registered each year, and many of those threats result in round-the-clock protection by deputy marshals.

Prisoner Custody and Transportation

The U.S. Marshals Service is responsible for the custody, housing, and transport of every prisoner of a federal agency. On any given day they have more than 28,000 prisoners in custody in federal or state jails. After conviction, marshals transport prisoners to their designated correctional institutions using their own fleet of airplanes: Con-Air for federal prisoners and the Justice Alien Transportation System for state prisoners. The latter is one of the largest transporters of prisoners in the world, moving approximately 200,000 prisoners a year.

Special Operations Group (SOG)

Deputy marshals volunteer to be specially trained for the Special Operations Group (SOG) tactical unit, one of the most elite response teams in the country. SOG carries out special missions throughout the United States and its territories, from protecting dignitaries to seizing assets to emergency response. Trained in tactics and weaponry, they also provide security to the Department of Defense and the U.S. Air Force during the transport of nuclear warheads. With the exception of some full-timers stationed at the William F. Degan Tactical Operations Center in Louisiana, SOG is a part-time assignment whose members are given regular deputy marshal work when they are not required for special duty.

Asset Seizure and Forfeiture

Under the Crime Control Act of 1984, the Marshals Service has the authority to seize assets related to investigations, primarily those involving drug trafficking, money laundering, organized crime, and fraud. This successful program allows criminal assets such as cars, boats, artwork, real estate, jewelry, and cash to be auctioned off once a court judgment has been rendered. The proceeds go into an asset forfeiture fund, which offsets the cost of criminal investigations by the marshals and other law enforcement agencies. While the benefits are enjoyed by many agencies, it is the sole responsibility of the marshals to inventory and maintain the seized property until final court decisions are rendered.

Judgment Enforcement Teams

Judgment Enforcement Teams receive special training to work with financial litigation units. Their purpose is to investigate and collect money owed the federal government including criminal fines and ill-gotten gains from federal fraud.

Becoming a U.S. Marshal

Qualifications

- U.S. citizen.
- Between the ages of twenty-one and thirty-seven at the time of hire.
- Pass the written tests.
- Pass the oral interview.
- Permit and then pass a background check.
- Bachelor's degree (criminal justice is helpful) or three years of law enforcement experience or a combination of education and experience.
- Pass the Fitness in Total Standards test, which includes sit-ups, push-ups, and a 1.5-mile run.
- Be willing to relocate to any district office.
- Vision no worse than 20/200, correctable to 20/20.

Salary

Starting salaries for deputy U.S. marshals range from $28,500 to $36,500 annually, depending on education and work experience.

The Specialists
Secret Service, Capitol Police, DEA, ATF, U.S. Customs, and Border Patrol

F EDERAL LAW ENFORCEMENT HAS MANY SPECIALIZED BRANCHES. This chapter focuses on several specialized agencies of experts.

■ THE SECRET SERVICE

The Secret Service is best known for protecting the president, vice president, and their families, so it comes as a surprise to learn that the agency is a branch of the Treasury Department and only became the official protectors of the president in 1906. Established in 1865, the Secret Service was originally formed to investigate and combat the rampant counterfeiting that took place as a result of the Civil War. In fact, at the war's end, fully one-third of circulating currency in the United States was counterfeit, creating a genuine emergency that put the country's financial stability at great risk.

While the service occasionally ventured into investigations of government land fraud, Ku Klux Klan activities, and counterespionage during the Spanish-American War, its primary focus was on the money supply until the assassination of President McKinley in 1901. The third president killed in thirty-six years, McKinley's death spurred Congress into action and resulted in the enactment of a law enabling the service to provide permanent presidential protection. These duties eventually expanded to include the first family, the vice president and family, former presidents and their families, primary candidates for these offices, and visiting dignitaries.

Those under Secret Service watch are known as "protectees." In order to safeguard Secret Service communications, protectees are given code names (the president, for instance, might be "Eagle"). Before their charges go anywhere, the Secret Service sends out an "advance team." These teams do a thorough investigation and sweep of their assigned destination, setting up command posts, coordinating communications with local, state, and federal law enforcement agencies, determining evacuation routes in case of emergency, putting fire and rescue workers on notice, determining necessary manpower, setting up checkpoints, and investigating threats or potential danger posed by hostile groups or individuals. Once the destination is deemed safe, the agents travel with and provide round-the-clock security for the president and other protectees.

Secret Service agents continue to be involved in financial investigations. Agents now investigate bank and credit-card fraud, computer crime, illegal electronic-funds transfers, falsification of government securities, and forgery and theft of U.S. treasury checks or bonds. Their forensic science division authenticates documents and currency along with other standard forensic-related matters.

Becoming a Secret Service Agent

Qualifications

Prospective Secret Service agents must meet the following requirements:

- U.S. citizen.
- Between the ages of twenty-one and thirty-seven at the time of appointment.
- Bachelor's degree from an accredited college or university; three years of work experience in criminal investigation or law enforcement; or a combination of the two.
- Vision no worse than 20/60 and correctable to 20/20.
- Excellent health.
- Pass the treasury enforcement agency examination.
- Submit to and pass a background examination that includes interviews, drug screening, a medical examination, and a polygraph test.

Salary

The beginning salary range is from $30,000 to $35,000 annually, dependent upon experience.

THE CAPITOL POLICE

Until two Capitol officers, Jacob Chestnut and John Gibson, lost their lives in 1998 protecting tourists and members of Congress from an armed intruder, this unit of the Secret Service was not much in the public eye. A force of 1,200 officers, the Capitol Police are charged with guarding the White House, the House of Representatives, the Senate, and all Capitol grounds.

Established in 1930 under Herbert Hoover after an unknown intruder walked unchallenged into the White House dining room, the Capitol Police, under the auspices of the Secret Service, took over duties previously discharged by military and metropolitan police. Since then, those responsibilities have expanded to the vice presidential residence, traveling members of Congress, and the visitor's galleries of the House and Senate.

Capitol Police have the same authority as any other law enforcement officer and are empowered to arrest anyone disrupting legislative proceedings. Divisions within the force include the hostage unit; the canine explosives detection unit; the emergency response team; special operations; crime-scene search technicians; and foot, bicycle, and car patrols.

Becoming a Capitol Police Officer

Qualifications

- U.S. citizen.
- Between the ages of twenty-one and thirty-seven at the time of hire.
- High-school diploma or equivalent.
- Excellent physical condition.
- Vision no worse than 20/60, correctable to 20/20.
- Submit to and pass a background check.
- Good driving record.
- Pass an oral interview and written test.
- Pass a drug screen and medical examination.
- Pass a polygraph test.

Salary

The beginning salary range for the Capitol Police uniformed division is $25,000 to $30,000 annually.

■ THE DRUG ENFORCEMENT AGENCY (DEA)

The Drug Enforcement Agency (DEA), a branch of the Justice Department, is the primary agency charged with the investigation and arrest of drug traffickers both in the United States and abroad.

Drug enforcement agents combat drug crimes in several ways. First, they enforce all drug laws. Second, they coordinate and cooperate with law enforcement agencies both here and abroad to monitor drug intelligence networks, combat distribution operations, assist in investigations, and arrest major and minor dealers. Third, they seize assets related to drug trafficking.

DEA Programs

DEA agents conduct their investigations through several programs:

Asset Forfeiture

Agents seize property and assets linked to drug-related crimes.

Aviation Operations

This program provides air assistance to federal, state, and local actions against drug traffickers.

Demand Reduction

Agents work in the field of drug-use prevention.

Diversion Control

This program inhibits the distribution of legal drugs for illegal use.

El Paso Intelligence Center

Created to serve as a strategic drug enforcement unit, particularly along the U.S./Mexico border, this center also serves as the training center for Operation Pipeline, a highway interdiction program.

Foreign Cooperation

This division works with foreign intelligence (with seventy-nine offices in fifty-six countries) conducting continuing investigations into drug trafficking in this country.

High-intensity Drug Trafficking Areas

This program is a coordinated effort with federal, state, and local law enforcement agencies to reduce drug trafficking in high-intensity areas.

Intelligence

Agents collect and disseminate vital information for fighting drugs to other federal, state, local, and foreign law enforcement organizations.

Laboratories

Technicians and laboratories located in New York City, Chicago, Miami, Dallas, San Francisco, and National City, Calif., McLean, Va., and Washington, D.C.—provide forensic services to all other branches of law enforcement.

Marijuana Education

This program has been established in fifty states to eradicate marijuana use.

Mobile Enforcement

This team, initiated in 1995, was developed in response to the increasing number of violent, drug-related crimes in major U.S. cities. Working closely with state and local law officials the team had arrested more than 7,000 criminals as of January 1999.

National Drug Pointer Index

This program monitors and coordinates information about current federal, state, and local drug investigations so that separate agencies may work cooperatively.

Organized-crime Drug Enforcement

This task force was created to promote the combined efforts of federal, state, and local law enforcement against drug trafficking by organized crime.

Becoming a DEA Agent

Qualifications

Prospective DEA agents must meet the following qualifications:
- U.S. citizen.
- Between the ages of twenty-one and thirty-six at the time of hire.
- Valid driver's license.
- College degree with a minimum 2.95 grade point average.
- Complete the special agent interview process that requires full disclosure of past drug use.
- Pass a polygraph test.

- Pass a psychological examination.
- Pass a physical fitness test.
- Vision correctable to 20/20 in one eye and 20/40 in the other.

Additionally, law enforcement experience counts, as does a willingness to move—DEA agents are transferred frequently and must be willing to accept assignments anywhere in the United States.

Salary

The beginning salaries for DEA agents range from $24,000 to $35,000 annually.

▓ THE BUREAU OF ALCOHOL, TOBACCO, AND FIREARMS (ATF)

Established in 1791, the Bureau of Alcohol, Tobacco, and Firearms (ATF) is a branch of the Treasury Department that was originally created as a tax-collecting agency. Since then the bureau's duties have expanded to include the investigation of federal law violations relating to firearms, explosives, arson, and the illegal trafficking of legal drugs and alcohol. Agents conduct surveillance and property raids, interview witnesses and suspects, procure search warrants, conduct searches, and make arrests. The ATF assists the U.S. attorney in preparing cases for trial and works closely with other law enforcement agents in task-force investigations.

The National Response Team (NRT) responds to all major bombing and fire scenes. Working both nationally and internationally, NRT units are composed of criminal investigators and explosives-technology and forensics experts. The ATF is a leader in forensic research (see chapter 8).

Becoming an ATF Agent

Qualifications

Prospective ATF agents must meet the following qualifications:

- U.S. citizen.
- Between the ages of twenty-one and thirty-seven at time of hire.
- Pass the treasury enforcement agent examination.
- Four-year college degree (courses useful toward becoming an ATF agent include criminal justice, forensic science, political science, chemistry, and accounting), or one year of work experience in the criminal justice field in addition to two years of criminal-investigation experience.
- Pass a medical examination.
- Vision no worse than 20/100, correctable to 20/30 in one eye.

Salary

The beginning salaries for ATF agents fall between $24,000 and $35,000 annually.

■ THE U.S. CUSTOMS SERVICE

The U.S. Customs Service special investigators are involved in cases of narcotics smuggling, child pornography, and money laundering; in the enforcement of the Arms Export Control Act;

and in combating the infringement of intellectual-property rights. They are also involved in air and marine drug-interdiction programs. Customs investigators are empowered to search without a warrant any person, baggage, car, or other conveyance crossing or approaching the U.S. border.

U.S. Customs special investigators employ any number of investigative techniques including physical and electronic surveillance, informants, examination of bank and import/export records, witness interviews, and search warrants. Additionally they work as interagency liaisons on multijurisdictional investigations.

Other jobs within the Customs Service include customs inspectors, pilots, and canine enforcement.

Becoming a Customs Service Special Investigator

Qualifications

Prospective Customs Service special investigators must meet the following requirements:

- U.S. citizen.
- No more than thirty-seven years old at the time of hire (this age limit is waived for federal law enforcement officers).
- Pass a personal background investigation.
- Accept assignments to any U.S. Customs location.

Salary

The salary for customs investigators begins at between $24,000 to $35,000 annually.

■ THE BORDER PATROL

This law enforcement agency is a branch of the Immigration and Naturalization Service (INS). Established in 1924, the basic mission of the Border Patrol has remained essentially unchanged: To detect undocumented illegal immigrants and prevent them from entering the country. Border Patrol duties have been expanded to aid in the combat of drug smuggling. Patrol agents are the primary drug-interdicting agency for all U.S. land ports of entry.

Agents conduct surveillance at land ports, interpret and collect physical evidence and intelligence information, respond to sensor alarms, and conduct traffic checks. Agents stationed at the border perform checkpoint duties. Those stationed in the interior generally perform city patrol duties, check farms and ranches, and monitor highway traffic.

Becoming a Border Patrol Agent

Qualifications

Prospective Border Patrol agents must meet the following requirements:

- U.S. citizen.
- Between the ages of twenty-one and thirty-seven at time of hire.
- Valid driver's license.
- Pass an entry-level test.
- Substantial previous work experience or a combination of education and work experience.
- Excellent physical condition.
- Agree and submit to a background investigation.

- Participate in an oral interview.
- Pass a drug screen.
- Test for binocular vision at 20/40 without corrective lenses.

Salary

Beginning salaries for Border Patrol agents range from $24,000 to $35,000 annually.

CHAPTER SEVEN

Training for the Front Lines

A LTHOUGH STATE AND LOCAL OFFICERS TRAIN IN DIFFERENT facilities than those at the federal level, all officers undergo rigorous training and must meet demanding standards of physical and academic performance as well as prove their ability to make sound judgments in extraordinarily difficult circumstances. This chapter outlines various training programs and offers advice from law enforcement professionals about what separates failed cadets from graduates and how best to continue advancing in your chosen branch of law enforcement.

■ THE POLICE ACADEMY: TRAINING AT THE STATE AND LOCAL LEVEL

Forget any goofy images this title might evoke from slapstick movie comedies of the same name—police academy training is tough. To receive certification as a peace officer, all recruits must complete Police Officer Standard Training (POST). Recruits generally live at the academy during the week (small jurisdictions unable to finance their own facilities send recruits to state training academies) and their daily activities range from staged physical encounters with suspects to class-room instruction on legal statutes and police procedures.

Training and Education

During approximately five months in the academy, recruits receive instruction on a variety of matters that can be broadly broken down into the following categories.

Patrol Operations

These include standard patrol procedure, vehicle and building search, use of backup patrols, felony stops and field interviews, crowd control, disaster preparedness, K-9 techniques, and various mock scenarios covering both day and night preparedness.

Criminal Investigations

Crime-scene protection and processing; crime prevention; forensics, including firearms identification, fingerprinting, and crime lab; and felony particulars, including sex crimes, domestic violence, narcotics, and property crime are all part of criminal investigations.

Safety and Wellness

This training includes physical conditioning; tactics and use of force; firearms, baton, and pepper-spray training; first aid and hazardous-material response; and critical-stress and mental-health alerts.

Communication Skills

Includes interrogation, crisis intervention, cultural diversity, report writing, and radio communications all considered communication skills.

Criminal Process

This category includes criminal, constitutional, and juvenile law; narcotics, liquor, and gambling statutes; the municipal code; and court testimony and protocol.

Traffic Enforcement

This category covers field sobriety and drug recognition, traffic control and direction, collision investigation, emergency-vehicle operation, and defensive driving.

Professional Responsibility and Community Policing

This category focuses on ethics, problem-solving, internal investigations, workplace relations, media relations, community service, and, ultimately, graduation preparation.

Gaining Admission to the Police Academy

Captain Michael T. Nault retired from the King County Police Department in 1994 but continues to consult for the department and several federal agencies and also lectures internationally on policing. He notes that the expectations of recruits about police work may differ from the day-to-day reality. Nault says statistics prove that the majority of police calls are service related and only a small percentage are what people typically think of as "law enforcement," such as arrest and pursuit or criminal investigations. Aspiring law enforcement officers must understand and respect these realities.

"Perceptions of police work that are gained from the sensationalism of media, TV, and movies are generally inaccurate and are quickly dispelled in police academy training," Nault says. "Too often, though, that perception is retained by the new officer and unhappiness or dissatisfaction with the career may follow. Therefore, the police selection process now holds as high criteria the candidate's ability and desire to work with other people. Those with underlying motives of power and control are ferreted out in the psychological and background examination process typical of any police hiring and training."

Many applicants must pass an oral interview as well as written tests. Deputy marshal Dennis Behrend suggests that during the oral interview, which consists of situational judgment questions, the responder should take their time answering and make sure to give specific and detailed answers. He stresses the importance of answering all background questions honestly, even if those answers (such as a revelation of drug use) may disqualify you.

Nault says it is not uncommon for law enforcement agencies to find themselves screening up to 250 candidates for any *one* available position just to meet the minimum required levels of background, integrity, and intelligence. "The public is extremely well served by these exacting selection processes. The result is officers who are highly intelligent, motivated, caring, and extraordinarily competent professionals."

Deputy sheriff candidates also train at the police academy but add to their curriculum training specific to sheriff department duties, such as serving warrants. These candidates must then pass an extensive oral review by a board from the sheriff's department. Once that is passed, deputies go on to the field training office where they ride with experienced deputies for three months, followed by solo duty that is monitored by experienced officers. New sheriffs' deputies are on one-year probation and only when that's done can their training period be considered complete.

State police officers also train at the police academy. Though they must be twenty-one years old to join the force, some high-school graduates become cadets and work behind the scenes in a primarily administrative capacity until they're old enough to join the force.

After Graduation: Education and Advancement

Graduation from the academy does not signal the end of a police officer's training. Changes in the law and technological advances in crime fighting make it imperative that officers stay up to date. Officers seeking advancement in rank must also pursue further education—both in and out of the department.

As noted earlier, special training in weapons, tactics, negotiations, and other skills are available within departments for those officers interested in special duties. Officers also study and test for advances in rank within the department. "Police ranks such as sergeant, lieutenant, and captain are managerial positions and carry with them those typical responsibilities," Nault says. "The TV and movie images of those ranks are inaccurate. The media would have you believe that those ranks represent police expertise, such as the better detective is a sergeant, and the even better one is a lieutenant. Those characterizations are not true. Police rank is accorded based on test-taking, and promotion is a result of an assessment of the person's capability to supervise or manage. It has nothing to do with that person's relative expertise at doing basic police work."

Advancement in the police ranks, just like anywhere else, may not always be equitable. Retired officer Mark Hurley of the San Francisco Police Department has concerns about the fact that written examinations and field experience are no longer the primary factors in promotion. "Now there are oral examinations, which are somewhat subjective to begin with, and often more indicative of an officer's freedom to study manuals than his job performance. You might have one officer who scores really well on the written and puts in a lot of time on the streets, another who spends a lot of time at his desk studying the materials that might impress the oral review board. Many times, that [the latter] officer gets the job and it causes a lot of resentment, particularly among those with higher written scores who aren't happy about reporting to a guy who lacks their general knowledge.

Officer Gary Lark is also concerned about the lack of common-sense testing, but in his small Michigan department that manifests itself in standardized testing, mass-produced exams designed for both small-town and urban police departments. "A lot of what they test for simply doesn't apply in a small-town setting, and those tests miss a lot of things that are important here."

For those seeking to advance their education, there are some interesting possibilities. After graduation from the University of Michigan, Lark received several job offers, among them security officer for Marquette University. Although Lark ultimately decided to stay in his hometown and work with its rapidly advancing department, the security job did offer an enticing perk. "Marquette would have provided continuing education for both me and my wife," Lark says. For officers trying to work a job and further their education, this may be an option worth pursuing.

Ranking officers clearly benefit from an education that combines study in the more general academic setting of a college or university with training at designated law enforcement academies. Chief of Police James Montgomery of the Bellevue, Washington Police Department, who regularly encourages his officers to continue their education, possesses a bachelor's degree in police administration and a master's degree in community development. He participated in both the FBI Law Enforcement Development Program and training at the FBI National Executive Institute. Seattle Sheriff David Reichert has a bachelor of science in sociology and a degree in forensic science. He attended Secret Service training on providing protection to the president and dignitaries. Montgomery, Reichert, and many others have taken advantage of the opportunity to study at federal training facilities, some of the best in the world.

▊ FLETC: TRAINING AT THE FEDERAL LEVEL

Most federal officers receive the majority of their instruction at the Federal Law Enforcement Training Center (FLETC). FLETC is the training ground for more than seventy federal law enforcement agencies. Located at a former Navy base in Glynco, Georgia, FLETC is an interagency training organization offering various levels of training. The core program at FLETC is basic investigative and uniformed police training. The next course level involves more specialized training for those wanting to advance beyond entry-level ranks. These courses run the gamut from law enforcement photography to wildfire investigation.

More than one hundred advanced training programs specific to various federal agencies are conducted through FLETC. Each program is custom-designed by the federal agency that sponsors it. Participating agencies include the ATF, Department of Justice, DEA, National Park Service, Bureau of Prisons, Marshal Service, Coast Guard, Customs Service, Department of the Mint, and Secret Service.

Modifying FLETC Training

Here are some of the ways in which federal agencies modify their FLETC training to meet specific needs:

Deputy Marshals

After sixteen weeks of general training, the last six weeks at the academy are agency-specific. Courses include fugitive investigation, prisoner transport, and protecting the courts. Marshals return to the academy every two or three years for two weeks of updated course training. There is also ongoing training available for those who want to join specialty units such as the Special Operations Group (SOG).

Even though marshals are considered one of the most highly trained groups in law enforcement, the U.S. Marshals are committed to modernizing and improving the organization, specifically in the area of training. U.S. Marshal Rosa Melendez, the highest-ranking woman of color in U.S. law enforcement, notes, "It is our policy to send all deputy marshals through refresher training every two to three years at FLETC. I also encourage our officers to pursue additional training and to participate in professional organizations."

Secret Service

After nine weeks of general course study in the Criminal Investigation Training Program (CITP) at FLETC, agents go on to eleven weeks of special training at the Secret Service's training academy in Beltsville, Maryland. Secret Service–specific training includes protective intelligence investigations, counterfeiting and other financial criminal activity, physical protection techniques, firearm training, and special tactics. The Capitol Police force also receives its training in the same FLETC division as the Secret Service, where officers are trained in police procedure, criminal law, search-and-seizure law, defense training, diplomatic immunity, international protocol, and first aid.

Customs Service International Training Division

Following FLETC basic training, these courses offer specialized training for foreign customs (and other law enforcement) in such areas as international narcotics interdiction, antiterrorism, money laundering, and international carrier initiatives.

Border Patrol

The extensive and rigorous nineteen-week training curriculum at FLETC covers topics such as immigration and nationality law, criminal law, border patrol operations, firearms, and physical training. Additionally, all agents must take an intensive Spanish course (Spanish fluency is not a prerequisite for admission).

ATF

These cadets undergo an eight-week course at FLETC and attend specialized new professional training, which covers topics such as federal firearm laws, arson investigation, evidence collection, bomb-scene search, and constitutional law. Each program includes oral and written examinations designed to test not only general knowledge but also communication skills, the ability to make judgments and adapt to differing situations, and individual integrity.

■ THE FBI ACADEMY

Probably the most extensive and specialized training in all of law enforcement is given to FBI agents. The training offered at the FBI academy in Quantico, Virginia, is the result of J. Edgar Hoover's vision of his agents as ideal law enforcement officers, highly trained and educated professionals.

Candidates enrolled at Quantico undergo fifteen weeks (654 hours) of intensive instruction. The training is divided into four sections: academics, firearms, physical training and defensive tactics, and practical exercises. Topics covered under these areas of study include behavioral and forensic sciences; interviewing and communications; investigation of white-collar crime and financial crimes; drug trafficking, organized crime; terrorism; and physical and defensive tactics.

The FBI academy is an enormous complex that covers more than 385 acres. In 1987, "Hogan's Alley," a mock town complete with banks, stores, cars, streets, and alleys, was added to provide a safe and private training ground for cadets and other law enforcement trainees. In this practical-application phase of the training, cadets participate in simulated terrorist attacks, hostage negotiations, bank robberies, and other crime scenarios. This is also an ideal location for perfecting firearm skills and continuing physical fitness training.

The FBI academy is noteworthy for the training it offers in computer crimes. Because of the complexity of computer forensic crimes, computer training at the academy varies from a basic course of study lasting a few weeks to extensive training that can take months. Academy computer training is utilized by all branches of law enforcement at the federal, state, and local levels.

DEA agents are also trained at Quantico, utilizing such assets as "Hogan's Alley." Their sixteen-week course covers basic criminology and investigative techniques; topics include use of firearms, ethics, drug identification, court procedure, and seizure and forfeiture laws.

New agents are placed on a two-year probationary period. The end of probation does not, however, signal the end of education.

Continuing Education and Training

Training, seminars, and workshops designed to hone and enhance a variety of skills are available to the agents (and other interested members of law enforcement) throughout their careers. Some of the additional training programs offered by the FBI include:

The FBI National Academy

This training program provides college-level training to state, local, and foreign police officers with an eleven-week course for mid-to-upper-level officers in areas such as management and behavioral sciences, forensics, hostage negotiations, and psychological profiling.

Operational Assistance Program

This program allows for FBI faculty to conduct research and assist other federal, state, and local law enforcement officers in specialized areas such as forensic hypnosis, psychological profiling, hostage negotiations, and major-case strategy.

Critical Incident Response Group (CIRG)

This organization promotes training and operational support specifically in the areas of terrorist activity, hostage taking, barricade situations, and other crisis situations requiring immediate or emergency response by multiple law enforcement officers. The FBI rescue team and field SWAT programs are part of CIRG.

National Center for the Analysis of Violent Crime (NCAVC)

This organization, formed in 1985, acts as a resource center providing research, training, and investigative and operational support to law enforcement agencies involved in major criminal investigations including serial killing, homicide, rape, child abduction, arson, hijacking and hostage negotiation.

Forensic Science Research and Training Center

This center trains FBI agents and other federal, state, and local law enforcement officers in techniques and procedures for handling and examining evidence to be used in court crimes.

International Instruction

This program allows FBI instructors to travel worldwide to teach topics such as organized and economic crime and nuclear nonproliferation.

▪ MILITARY TRAINING FOR CIVILIAN SERVICE

Retired San Francisco Police Department officer Mark Hurley believes that military training is a real advantage for those considering a career in civilian law enforcement. "When I became an officer military service was still mandatory. With one exception, every man in academy class had already gone through military training. They knew how to take orders and direction and they knew how to work together. It made a real difference."

For those considering a career in law enforcement but may not be able to afford college classes or would like some practical experience before making a career decision, the military is an excellent option.

Military investigations offer long-term careers, and for those who desire a return to civilian life, most federal or local law enforcement agencies offer special consideration to those who have served in the military.

Military Training Options

Several military branches offer training related to civilian law enforcement.

The Coast Guard

Mostly involved in environmental protection, national security, and search and rescue, the Coast Guard's maritime enforcement division is on the front lines of the drug war as the leading agency for maritime interdiction of illegal drugs. Partnered with the U.S. Customs Service, the Coast Guard assists with negotiations pertaining to bilateral drug prevention agreements with Caribbean countries and conducts drug interdiction efforts. This division is responsible for more than 25 percent of cocaine and marijuana seizures.

The Coast Guard also has a law enforcement branch through the Coast Guard Investigations (CGI) office and a police division. The Coast Guard offers excellent preparation for a career in law enforcement, particularly the special harbor-patrol unit. There are four ways to join the Guard: by enlisting; by meeting the special qualifications to become a commissioned officer; by enrolling in a free, four-year course of college study at the Coast Guard academy; or by a part-time commitment to the Coast Guard reserves.

U.S. Army Criminal Investigation Command (CID)

CID officers are responsible for investigating crimes, ranging from murder to drug violations to fraud, that relate to the Army and its interests. These active military personnel also perform protective duties for the Secretary of Defense, Secretary of the Army, and other officials and dignitaries. CID officers must have a minimum of two years' service, including six months with the military or one year with civilian police, or six months as an intern with a CID unit. They receive training at Quantico, FLETC, and sometimes Scotland Yard.

The Military Police

They are responsible for maintaining and enforcing laws on military bases. They also provide security for VIPs, military banks, harbors, and ports. In cases of extreme disaster or unrest, MPs may be called upon to help restore order. In wartime, MPs are the front line of defense against terrorism. They also secure special ammunition and guard and evacuate prisoners of war. All enlisted members of the military are qualified to become MPs. During a ten-week training course at the military training school in Fort McClang, potential MPs are instructed in subjects such as defensive tactics, investigations, and law enforcement situations.

Naval Criminal Investigative Service (NCIS)

This primary investigation unit for the Navy also conducts counterintelligence and manages the Navy's security program. The staff is combined military and civilian personnel, stationed at more than 150 locations around the world as well as on aircraft carriers. These officers investigate homicide, rape, burglary, robbery, theft, and any other crimes occurring on naval bases or aboard ships at sea or in port.

NCIS special agents train at FLETC—first a nine-week basic criminal-investigation course, then an additional six weeks of NCIS-specific training. Throughout their careers NCIS officers continue to train on such subjects as death investigation, child-molester profiling, rape, blood-borne pathogens, and crime-scene processing. Civilian careers within the agency include chemistry, forensic science, electronics, computers, and intelligence.

■ FINDING JOBS ON THE FRONT LINE

At the local level, there is a centralized place to find not only law enforcement jobs but also all civil-service positions currently available. The civil service job board is generally found in the city or town hall of virtually every town. These boards list every availability, from senior law enforcement to file clerk, and offer instruction as to where to apply, what qualifications are needed, and which examinations are required.

More and more, individual departments at both the state and federal levels are listing job opportunities on their Web sites. If a home computer is not available, local libraries often have free Internet service. For a nominal fee, many copy shops rent computer access by the hour.

To investigate law enforcement careers, students may wish to participate in an internship program through their college or university. Others considering law enforcement may find that participating in a police-sponsored volunteer program can clarify if this is the field for them (volunteer experience also serves a candidate well when competing for a place in academy training). To find out about the opportunities in your area, call the department's community relations office. Volunteer opportunities may include:

• Neighborhood surveillance.
• Video surveillance.

- Ham watch (radio surveillance). Volunteers must be licensed ham radio operators.
- Graffiti abatement.
- Station assistance, including general office and clerical duties.
- At-risk youth programs.
- Crisis response.
- Neighborhood watch.

Scene of the Crime

A BODY HAS BEEN LOCATED, THE SCENE SECURED BY A patrolman, a detective called to the location. Now it's time for the crime-scene specialists to take over, to document the position of the body, whether it is sprawled on a bed or slumped over in the front seat of a car. They chart any disruptions at the scene, such as a house's overturned furniture or fresh tire tracks on a deserted road. Photographs and video are taken by the detectives or an assigned photographer. Visible prints are photographed, and a latent-print specialist dusts every likely surface for prints hidden to the naked eye. Meanwhile, a medical examiner checks the body for obvious clues to cause of death and then, after detectives chalk the outline of the corpse's position, sends it off to the morgue for an autopsy. Nearby, lab technicians check the scene inch by inch, searching for hair or drops of blood that could reveal the suspect's DNA and confirm his identity; carpet or clothing fibers that might be used to track the suspect; or anything that could provide a link to the perpetrator of the crime.

This evidence is carefully labeled and recorded, the detective returns to his station and checks it into custody, and then it is ready to be studied by the scientific detectives known as forensic experts.

Detail-oriented and dedicated to uncovering truths buried in evidence most of us don't care to think about, forensic specialists are genuine crime-fighting heroes.

In a criminal justice system whose participants may sometimes rush to judgment, the cool, objective eye of the forensic scientist does much to safeguard justice. Unlike cops or attorneys, whose personal interactions with the victims and criminals may sometimes color their decisions, forensic specialists deal with scientific facts arrived at through chemical and biological analysis, examination of evidence, and "listening" carefully to the voice of the victim that speaks through the clues left behind on the body.

Forensic scientists must be curious, detail-oriented, meticulous, professional, educated, and continuously involved in the learning process, as new techniques that advance and refine their specialties are discovered nearly every day.

This section delves into the work of the physical and psychological clue finders who do their work based on the bits and pieces gathered at the scene of the crime.

CHAPTER EIGHT

Examining the Bodies of Evidence

Criminalists, Forensic Specialists, Coroners, and Medical Examiners

O NCE THE CRIME-SCENE EVIDENCE HAS BEEN COLLECTED IT IS turned over to a variety of forensic specialists. According to Webster's dictionary, "forensic" is defined as "involving the application of scientific, especially medical, knowledge to legal matters." Forensic scientists are vital to the criminal justice system. Their skills are employed by both prosecution and defense teams, as well as during the police investigation of the crime.

Most police departments operate their own crime labs staffed by forensic specialists. Forensic scientists also work for private facilities that may be contracted by the defense or as a "neutral party" agreed upon by both sides to handle difficult or questionable evidence.

Kay Sweeney now heads just such a lab, KMS Forensics. A forensic scientist since 1966, he began in the Seattle Police Department's crime laboratory and retired years later while managing several statewide programs in Washington State's criminal laboratory headquarters. A veteran of thousands of investigations, Sweeney's focus in the private sector has moved from conducting crime scene investigations and reconstructions for the police to working for the defense. While detectives have complete access to forensic investigations at no cost, the defense must pay a private forensic source. Sweeney says his employer in no way affects the outcome of his analysis. "My philosophy is that the forensic investigation should be free of bias. When I conduct an examination the result will be the same regardless of who is requesting the work."

The FBI's laboratory division is one of the largest and most comprehensive in the world. The well-funded labs are staffed with a remarkable variety of forensic experts including chemical, DNA, trace evidence and latent fingerprint, firearms and ballistics, surveillance photography and document examination, crime-scene experts, and polygraph examiners. The FBI also employs some unique specialists such as forensic experts in feather or soil analysis. All members of the FBI laboratory division consult on cases for other law enforcement agencies in addition to their federal duties and many of their specialists conduct training sessions for state and local crime-lab specialists and law enforcement officers. Additionally, these experts work with FBI agents in the disaster squad, a special team assembled to aid in the identification of the deceased at major disaster sites.

In smaller labs budgets are constrained, so most forensic specialists employed by them have multiple areas of expertise. Known as criminalists, theirs is the science of analysis, identification, comparison, and interpretation of physical evidence.

Rounding out the forensics field are those who deal with the remains of the deceased: medical examiners, coroners, pathologists, and human forensic specialists—for example, forensic anthropologists, who are able to determine age, sex, and cause of death from even decades-old skeletal remains.

■ THE CRIMINALIST

The criminalists who run police crime labs use their knowledge of physical and natural sciences to examine evidence, which can provide clues about how a crime was committed or whether a crime was committed at all. Skilled in most areas of forensic sciences, the criminalist reconstructs the crime scene, testing to identify hair, fibers, blood and semen stains, alcohol, drugs, paint, soil samples, and firearm and tool markings, all of which can be used to identify suspects in a crime. Their findings can support or disprove witness testimony, establish the suspect's whereabouts, and sometimes free a person wrongly accused. Criminalists are often expert witnesses who are regularly called to testify in court.

Types of Analysis Conducted by Criminalists

A proficient criminalist may conduct a variety of tests, or specialists may work individually and then share their findings to create a complete crime scene. Forensic investigations regularly utilize the work of the following specialists:

Biochemical Analysts

Biochemical analysts test for body fluids such as blood, semen, and saliva. These tests include traditional blood-typing protocols; they also determine whether the fluids belong to the victim, suspected perpetrator, or other individual; and what species the samples are from—human or some other animal (when bodies are found outdoors, animal contamination is often an issue). The analysts also evaluate and interpret the cause and content of stains. For example, a biochemical analyst is able to determine if the blood spot on a suspect's shirt arrived there as result of innocent contact with the victim (which might occur, for example, if the suspect attempted first aid) or as a blood-spatter deposit (which could indicate that the suspect stabbed the victim).

Chemical Analysts

They examine physical evidence for controlled-substance content (the presence of drugs, both legal and illegal, and alcohol) and other chemical substances (to determine whether a stain is gas, oil, or lighter fluid, for example). They also test compounds such as arson accelerants and explosives, which can be typed and identified from examination of the crime-scene residue.

DNA Identification Section Analysts

These specialists perform a more specialized function of biochemical analysis. These analysts identify human DNA found on evidence and calculate the statistical probability of it belonging to the suspect. The possibility of someone matching a DNA sample that doesn't belong to them is one in millions, or even billions, so there is a real finality to a DNA test that either identifies or excludes the person tested. DNA has proved a boon both for those charged with catching criminals and for those wrongly accused or incarcerated. Men trying to deny rape or sexual contact have a difficult time lying when the DNA left by their own blood, saliva, semen, hair, or skin provides such strong evidence. Conversely, the wrongly accused are safe from even the most insistent victim's testimony when

DNA rules out their presence at the crime scene. A number of convicted criminals have been able to prove their innocence with the help of organizations such as The Innocence Project, run by attorney Barry Scheck, an expert in dealing with DNA evidence. Tests of crime-scene samples, which were not technologically possible at the time of conviction, sometimes support a convict's repeated assertion that he did not do it. Frequently, however, DNA tests only confirm the court's verdict and prove yet again that the criminal is indeed guilty.

Fingerprint Technicians

Fingerprints can be retrieved during many phases of the criminal investigation. Detectives work with technicians from the latent print unit to uncover prints at the crime scene. While some prints are readily visible (bloody or greasy prints, for example), latent-print specialists uncover prints invisible to the human eye by chemically "dusting" for prints in areas likely to have been touched by the perpetrator such as windowsills, door frames, and doorknobs. Other fingerprints may be found on evidentiary items and are often discovered during thorough examinations in the police crime lab. Fingerprints can also be found on the victim; severe bruises may reveal a print, or prints may be briefly visible on skin as a result of surface oils.

Prints are retrieved through a variety of substances, such as dye stains, chemical developers, lasers, powder techniques, and quick-drying superglue, which capture the unique shape and ridges of fingerprints.

Once the print is recovered, it's compared to the hundreds of thousands of prints available on the statewide computer database called the Automated Fingerprint Identification

System (AFIS), which has revolutionized law enforcement. States can also coordinate with the Federal Bureau of Investigation's national AFIS database to compare fingerprints with those collected in every state.

The AFIS database is kept current through the efforts of fingerprint technicians. On a local level they are generally employed and overseen by sheriffs' departments. These units include:

The jail identification unit. This unit operates seven days a week, twenty-four hours a day. The technicians fingerprint and photograph every inmate brought into the jail. These clear, readable prints make accurate identification efficient and easy for later matches and identification.

The ten-print unit. They process fingerprint cards on file to verify inmate identities and search for outstanding warrants. Qualifications for this job include having worked as a jail identification technician for one year, computer literacy, being detail-oriented, good communication skills, and the ability to work in a precise and comprehensive manner.

The latent print unit. This group processes prints, collects evidence from crime scenes, and gives testimony in court. By definition a latent print is one that can only be recovered by using powder or chemicals. Basic qualifications include two years' employment as a ten-print identification specialist; a two- or four-year degree, preferably in forensic science; and solid computer and communication skills.

The Integrated Automated Fingerprint Identification System (IAFIS). This system is a federal fingerprint database. With more than 215 million fingerprints on file it provides one national source where law enforcement agencies may retrieve and compare fingerprints from other states' databases for identification purposes.

Firearm and Toolmark Identification Specialists

These specialists determine the make, model, and caliber of the guns involved in a crime, and then determine the involvement of a specific firearm. Firearm specialists match the bullet to the gun that was fired by identifying toolmark characteristics. By using a microscope, specialists study the "rifling" (the marks left by specific grooves, nicks, and other variations in the rifle barrel at the time of firing) on the expended bullet. No two firearms leave the same rifling marks, so if the bullet is intact the analyst can confirm or eliminate a weapon as being involved in a particular crime. These analysts also conduct "proximity tests," which determine the distance of the firearm from its "striking point" such as the victim or a wall, fence, or furniture hit by random or misdirected fire.

Toolmark evidence may also be found on other potential weapons, such as nicks in a knife or splinters of a bat. These contribute to identifying the item as the one involved in the crime.

Microanalysts

These specialists evaluate microscopic physical evidence. High-powered instruments enable microanalysts to effectively examine tiny samples such as hair, carpet fiber, paint, or glass particles.

Imprint Evidence Specialists

They examine things like tire tracks and shoe prints for evidentiary purposes. Often working through the process of elimination, these experts first determine the general nature of a print, then track each ridge and groove to its specific identification, details of production, and, perhaps, availability. Some shoes are far rarer than others (such as the famous Bruno Magli shoes whose sole prints in O. J. Simpson's shoe size were found at the Nicole Simpson crime scene, but which were not definitively linked to him), and some prints reveal extremes in shoe size, both of which make tracking the footprint's owner a much more straightforward process. If the suspect and his shoes are already in custody, an imprint match can do much to convince a jury that they were indeed at the scene of the crime.

Questioned Document Evidence Specialists

These specialists cover a broad area of analysis including handwriting, forgery, and counterfeiting. Handwriting specialists study the formation of letters, the spacing between letters and words, and other unique markings. Counterfeiting specialists check for bill markings, ink coloration, paper thickness, watermarks, paper density, and other testing features designed into U.S. currency.

Forensic Computer Specialists

They analyze all aspects of computer use for tracing evidence to track and expose hackers, retrieve deleted communications such as e-mail, and retrieve files and other materials that may have been deleted from a computer hard drive.

Toxicology Experts

Toxicology experts analyze blood and/or urine to determine the levels of alcohol or controlled substances present at the time of the crime. When the cause of illness or death is in question, toxicologists may use their expertise to determine and identify the presence of poison or other harmful chemicals. Toxicologists are often called in when a victim has overdosed on drugs.

▓ MEDICAL EXAMINER AND CORONER'S OFFICES

Although their duties, skills, and training vary in some important ways, medical examiners and coroners begin every assignment in the same way—they arrive at the scene and make the pronouncement of death.

The Coroner's Office

The coroner is the public official responsible for making and entering into the public record the official pronouncement of death. The coroner signs the death certificate. Without this official document, no action can be taken having to do with assets, insurance, or wrongful-death claims regarding the deceased. This centralized process of registering deaths diminishes the potential for fraud.

Coroners are often elected and in rural areas may also serve as sheriffs. Coroners generally do not have medical backgrounds, so they do not personally determine the cause of death but rather are the official recorders of it. For instance, if police are summoned when someone has died of apparently natural causes, the officer's first call would be for an ambulance. The medical technicians would pronounce the person dead, and only then would the coroner be called. The coroner oversees removal of the body from the place of death. Unless the deceased was under the care of a doctor within the last ninety-two hours, a mandatory autopsy is ordered by the coroner.

The Medical Examiner

Unlike a coroner, the medical examiner (ME) is trained as a physician and brings this medical expertise to the investigation. The ME visits the crime scene, determines the cause of death or need for an autopsy, performs the autopsy, conducts a follow-up investigation, and testifies in court.

Jerry Webster, chief medical investigator for King County, Washington, estimates that in the nine years he's worked with the office he's personally investigated between 1,200 and 1,500 deaths. Webster supervises eleven medical investigators and oversees a staff that includes examiners and investigators, autopsy assistants, and support staff.

To Webster, an ideal candidate for employment has a four-year degree in health sciences and a minor in criminal justice. "The jobs here are very complex so we look for people who have a strong background in medical training and some investigative ability. It's very difficult to find these combinations in a potential hire. We like about 70 percent medical and 30 percent investigative background. This is a great field to pursue because people with those specific qualifications are rare, so those who possess them have great opportunities to advance."

Like the U.S. Marshals, medical examiners have a high success rate when it comes to "getting their man," in their case identifying the deceased. In Webster's years of service, his office has been unable to identify only about thirty individuals.

Medical examiners need not be specialists in pathology. They are, however, encouraged to train in death investigation. The National Association of Medical Examiners and the American Academy of Forensic Sciences are among those that offer training for medical examiners.

■ PATHOLOGY AND FORENSIC SPECIALISTS

For forensic pathologists and specialists, death does not end an individual's ability to speak. Through these specialists, the dead can tell their story and often bring the culpable to justice.

Pathologist

A forensic pathologist is a medical doctor specially trained in establishing causes of death. Their general focus is on soft tissue, including the analysis of organs, flesh, and body fluids. They perform their duties through a variety of laboratory examinations. Forensic pathologists are trained to perform autopsies, although doctors without this specialized degree may conduct autopsies as well. The autopsy procedure involves the taking of tissue biopsies, body-fluid cultures, and X rays, and rendering toxicological analysis. During a law enforcement investigation the forensic pathologist collects medical evidence, reconstructs the events leading to injury, and documents evidence of sexual assault and trauma. These experts are also trained in nonmedical disciplines such as trace evidence, ballistics, and DNA technology.

Once an autopsy is completed, a file is assembled containing the examination results, including victim photographs, toxicology results, injury X rays, and other materials supporting the determination of cause of death. These files play a vital role in investigation and their accuracy may be a defining factor in a successful prosecution.

The circumstances of death that require an autopsy include:

• Suspected homicide.
• Suicide.
• Unclear cause of death.

- Sudden death (unexplained death of someone apparently in good health).
- Unexpected death (such as a terminal illness that kills the patient much sooner than medically supported).

Forensic Specialists

Some individual remains require specialists to identify them. For example, a body destroyed by explosion or fire, or the remains of a horribly mutilated victim, can leave investigators clueless as to their identity. These types of cases require forensic specialists whose crime scene is the human body and the clues every single one carries inside.

Forensic Odontologists

They employ dental charts to identify or confirm the identity of an otherwise unrecognizable body. A forensic dentist can quickly compare a victim's charts from the family dentist with the dental X rays of the deceased to confirm or deny their identity. When the victim is completely unknown, dental forensics can help to determine age and offer clues such as bridgework, special fillings, or orthodontia, which link the body to known missing persons or send the detectives to dental specialists who may recognize their own handiwork.

Forensic odontologists also work with bite marks, which may be found on rape, murder, and assault victims, or on food. More often than expected, criminals stop after their "labors" for a sandwich, and that bite could lead to a positive identification.

Forensic Anthropologists

They work to identify skeletal remains. Forensic anthropology is a subfield of physical anthropology. An applied science, it borrows methods and techniques from skeletal biology and osteology (study of the skeleton) and uses them to assess the age, sex, physical stature, and ancestry of the deceased, along with the trauma, disease, or details of an attack. Such details are then entered into the National Crime Information Center (NCIC) database to see if they match descriptions of missing persons. Forensic anthropologists may also use computer enhancements to reconstruct a face. These facial reproductions may then be released via the media and can result in the identification of the corpse.

Forensic Entomologists

These specialists apply the study of insects and other arthropods to legal issues including murder, suicide, and rape but also relating to physical abuse and drug trafficking. It takes approximately two days in standard conditions for a corpse to reach the point of decay wherein it emits an odor that attracts flies. By noting the development of insects, the entomologist can predict with astonishing accuracy exactly when the person died. Insects may also reveal whether the body has been moved or the presence of toxins if the body is too decayed to produce useful samples. Maggots may be tested for the presence of drugs, poisons, or other toxic substances. In some horrible cases, the insects themselves may have been used as weapons.

Becoming a Forensic Science Professional

Qualifications

To qualify for a starting position in any forensics field the minimum requirement is a bachelor of science degree in chemistry, physics, or any of the natural sciences. Forensic specialist Kay Sweeney recommends a chemistry degree: "Anyone with a scientific background will be qualified to work in a police crime lab, but chemistry is a science that is somewhat investigative. A great part of lab work is being given unknowns and coming up with answers. Chemistry is a science where you are constantly asking questions and solving problems."

In addition to a degree, applicants are required to take a written test that examines such basic skills as math and reading comprehension. Study guides that may be useful are those geared toward SAT or GRE preparation, many of which are published by Barrons and Arco.

Forensic specialties require advanced degrees. For forensic anthropology, for example, the desired course of study would include an undergraduate degree in anthropology with courses in cultural anthropology, archaeology, and physical/biological anthropology as well as linguistics, genetics, biology, and other science courses. Graduate studies would then focus on forensic or applicable courses such as osteology or skeletal biology.

Salary

Entry-level salaries for forensic science professionals are between $28,000 and $32,000 annually.

Training

Candidates for employment as forensic lab technicians must have a bachelor of science degree in chemistry, physics, or any of the natural sciences. The position also requires some study of or practical experience in criminal justice, law, and the basic philosophy of forensic science.

With these skills in place, a candidate moves on to specialized training, whether on the job, in an internship capacity, or in academia. Facilities that provide such training include:

- The FBI Science Research and Training Center at Quantico, Virginia.
- Institutions such as the California Criminalistic Institute, a unit of the California Department of Justice, which provides more than fifty specialized training classes for forensic scientists including crime-scene and casework review. Classes are free to qualified California residents, and available to those from out of state for a fee of $500 per week.
- Private training facilities such as the Pacific Coast Forensic Institute or the National Forensics Science Center, which offer both short- and long-term training. Fees vary.
- Individual police departments that offer advanced training to the officers, either through the department or recognized adjunct training facilities. Colleges and universities offer forensic training, which varies by institution.

CHAPTER NINE

Inside the Criminal Mind
Profilers, Forensic Psychiatrists,
Criminologists, and Polygraph
Examiners

T HE FILM *THE SILENCE OF THE LAMBS* PROPELLED THE ROLE OF
the FBI profiler into the national consciousness. While
the story centers around rookie profiler Clarice Starling, the
character of her boss is based on real-life FBI profiler John
Douglas, whose books and interviews have given the public
inside information on this fascinating job.

Douglas and fellow profiler Ron Hazelwood first made
names for themselves, and proved the value of profiling, by
solving the Atlanta child murders in the 1980s. Poor black
children were being murdered in Atlanta; six were dead when
Hazelwood joined the hunt, and the number had risen to
sixteen when Douglas joined a short time later. Rumors
abounded that white racists were responsible. But Hazelwood
noticed that his very presence (as a white male) cleared the
streets where the children had been abducted, despite the fact
that he was accompanied by three black officers. He knew the

killer had to be black. No white person would have gone unnoticed approaching the children.

Douglas and Hazelwood pieced together a portrait of a black man in his twenties who, among other traits, related easily with children and sought media attention by leaving his victims in obvious sites. Tracking his patterns enabled the profilers to predict where the next body might be left—the local river bank. Indeed, after an interval of no activity, a body was tossed into the river and Wayne Williams was stopped near the scene. A twenty-three-year-old black man, he was regularly involved with children at the auditions he ran in a supposed attempt to put together the "next" Jackson 5. Though not arrested, Williams was under surveillance from that night on and eventually enough evidence was gathered to take him into custody. Williams was nearly identical to the description created by the behavioral scientists. The profilers' insights came in handy one more time in the Williams case. Day after day, Williams appeared in court as a mild-mannered figure seemingly incapable of violent murder. But when he got on the stand, Williams was submitted to a low-key yet relentless examination by the prosecution—a style of questioning suggested by the profilers to push Williams to erupt—and he did. Suddenly, the jury saw an angry, out-of-control defendant and they convicted him.

▉ PROFILERS

Profiling arose from the efforts of the FBI's Behavioral Science Unit. When law enforcement agencies from around the country found themselves stumped on an unsolved case, they would contact the FBI for assistance. These unsolved cases were then sent to the Behavioral Science Unit, whose agents looked for evidence pointing to the criminal. This type of predator identification was not immediately embraced or publicized by FBI officials, many of whom considered the work psychological "mumbo-jumbo."

With its success in the Atlanta case, the Behavioral Science Unit began to expand its knowledge through lengthy interviews with incarcerated serial killers, sexual sadists, and rapists, who provided hours of information about how and why they committed their crimes.

From these interviews, and their lengthy experience, profilers have compiled a checklist to help them put together a description of the predator they're seeking. They want to know:

- Age.
- Sex.
- Race.
- Where they live. (poor or middle class? urban or rural?)
- Level of intelligence.
- Occupation. (manual labor? skilled or unskilled? white collar?)
- Employment history. (one employer for years? drift from job to job? receive public assistance?)
- Marital status.
- Living arrangement. (with partner? parent? friends? alone?)
- Psycho-sexual maturity. (can they have normal sexual relations? a long-term relationship? do they have any physical problems? passive or dominant?)
- Type and condition of vehicle.
- Probable motivating factor.
- Arrest record. (is this person leading a seemingly "normal" life or do they have a history of trouble?)
- How to interrogate them after capture. (friendly? threatening? conspiratorial?)

These methods have a remarkable success rate, but not 100 percent. One case that was never solved still haunts every law officer involved: the Green River murders. More than forty women, mostly prostitutes, were killed and their bodies dumped along Seattle's Green River. There was almost no forensic evidence, and nothing to enable agents to create a profile. Surprisingly, serial killer Ted Bundy contributed reams of information about how he was able to lure his victims and evade capture.

The case took its toll on profiler John Douglas, who collapsed from encephalitis and required a five-month recovery period. Bill Hagmeir, director of FBI profiling, says such a physical collapse is not uncommon. "I've never seen a prolonged and complex case where one or two people didn't go down one way or another."

Those who work as profilers often give up a lot in their personal lives, but the job has real and profound rewards. The predators tracked by profilers don't stop on their own; they must be stopped. Profilers would agree that the family strain, the dark view of life, and the demanding hours are worth it for the lives they save.

Profilers work in both public and private facilities. Former FBI profiler Robert Kessler, one of the originators of FBI profiling guides, now works in private practice as a criminologist offering expert witness testimony, consultation for films and television, and expert commentary. Private-practice criminologists may also be hired by families of missing or deceased persons. John Douglas himself became the subject of some controversy when he released a profile excluding JonBenet Ramsey's parents as her possible murderers based on forensic details provided by her parents.

Becoming a Profiler

Qualifications

As profiling is not yet a skill that can be acquired by degree, there is no set path to becoming a profiler. Two specific sets of skills are required: knowledge of criminal justice and knowledge of psychology. Most originators of profiling worked their way up in the ranks. An undergraduate degree in psychology and law enforcement training combine to offer a sound basis for a career in profiling. Sam Houston University in Texas offers a very close link between their psychology and criminal justice colleges, and is a model for programs being created to address the growing field of profiling.

Salary

FBI profilers are agents who are paid on the same scale. Well-known profilers who provide media and private consultations can make considerably more money.

■ FORENSIC PSYCHIATRISTS AND PSYCHOLOGISTS

A psychiatrist sits with a distraught patient who describes how he felt when his wife told him in detail about the ten men she'd slept with after letting them watch her undress in the living room of the home she and her husband share. This is a man you might feel sympathy for until you learn that at the time his wife was supposedly telling him this, he was depositing her head in a public trash can, from which, he claimed, she continued to talk. Meanwhile, her mother was discovering her torso on the living room couch.

It might not seem to take a professional to determine that anyone who thinks a severed head is talking to him isn't fit to stand trial (and in this case, the defendant truly was insane). Unfortunately, criminals are often well versed, or believe they are, in feigning mental illness to avoid life in prison. For example, Kenneth Bianchi, one of the infamous "Hillside Stranglers," tried this strategy and nearly got away with it. Bianchi, along with his cousin Angelo Buono, was responsible for the rape, torture, and murder of more than a dozen young Los Angeles–area women, whose bodies they subsequently dumped in the surrounding hills.

When Buono decided the two should split up to avoid being caught, Bianchi moved to Washington state. He was unable to keep his impulses in check and murdered two girls. However, without Buono's assistance Bianchi left a mass of clues and was quickly arrested.

Bianchi may have been vicious, but he wasn't stupid, and he hatched a plan to get himself off. He had studied psychology and was able to convince his attorney that he was suffering from amnesia; then a psychiatric social worker suggested he must have multiple-personality disorder and Bianchi ran with this diagnosis.

Ultimately, however, experts in psychiatry testified that Bianchi was competent to stand trial, and he received life in prison.

Sometimes, people who are innocent may claim to be guilty, for a variety of psychological reasons. It is the job of the forensic psychiatrist or psychologist to assist in determining the mental state of the defendant or suspect, and how best for the prosecution to proceed.

Forensic psychiatrists and psychologists function in much the same way within the criminal justice system. Psychiatry is a medical subspecialty, while psychology is a science that does not require medical training. Psychiatrists are primarily called to consult on specific cases, offering medical diagnoses and determining whether an injury or medical condition could be a factor in a suspect's behavior. Psychologists are more likely to provide broad-based consultation on areas such as jury selection, maintaining order in prisons, and the screening and evaluation of prospective law enforcement officers as well as consultations on individual cases.

Both psychiatrists and psychologists provide their services in correctional institutions and psychiatric hospitals. Each profession may further specialize, such as offering intervention for troubled children and treatment for youth offenders. In prisons they may be called in to evaluate the offender's readiness for parole and chances for recidivism. When the finding is "not guilty by reason of insanity" their analysis may be the determining factor that sets the perpetrator free or keeps them institutionalized for years, or even life.

Becoming a Forensic Psychiatrist or Psychologist

Qualifications

Forensic psychiatrists must earn a basic medical degree, followed by advanced psychiatric studies. Forensic psychologists must have an undergraduate degree in basic psychology followed by specialized graduate work.

Salary

Salaries for forensic psychologists are between $42,000 and $64,000 annually. Salaries for forensic psychiatrists are between $55,000 and $86,000 annually.

Training

An undergraduate degree in psychology, graduate studies, and supervised practical experience are all qualifying factors for forensic psychology. Graduate students in psychology do hands-on clinical work including sessions with prison inmates. Subjects covered during undergraduate and graduate instruction leading to a forensic psychology degree include:

- Abnormal psychology.
- Psychometric testing.
- Social psychology.
- Personality.
- Criminology.
- Forensic science.

CRIMINOLOGISTS

Criminology is the scientific study of crime. Criminologists study the sociological and psychological factors involved in the causes and prevention of crime, as well as in criminal punishment and rehabilitation. Criminologists provide essential information to lawmakers, criminal-justice officials, corrections officers, and others involved in criminal justice.

Criminologists work in a variety of venues. In an academic setting they may track trends in criminal behavior and catalogue the socioeconomic factors that contribute to those trends. In the private sector they advise on matters ranging from prisoner counseling to community policing. In the criminal justice system they counsel other professionals on a range of issues, including drug abuse and its effects; environmental factors that may contribute to violent crime; variances in the criminal justice system related to race and ethnicity; and the cause and effect of childhood abuse and later criminal behavior.

Criminologists frequently combine their efforts with those of other professionals such as sociologists, psychologists, and anthropologists to produce the most complete and well-rounded data possible.

Becoming a Criminologist

Qualifications

Criminologists must have a master's degree and preferably a Ph.D. in criminal justice or criminology. Given that much of the job entails conducting interviews and gathering data, they should also have good people skills and a lively and investigative mind.

Salary

The salary range of criminologists is between $28,000 and $45,000 annually.

Training

Criminologists have many options for advanced training. The following organizations sponsor workshops and seminars where a myriad of subjects related to criminology are covered, such as victimology, crime statistics, criminal justice trends, gang violence, and the impact and effectiveness of the jail system. The fees for membership and conferences vary. Contact the following organizations for more information:

American Society of Criminology
1314 Kinnear Road
Columbus, OH 43212-1156
(614) 292-9207

Western Society of Criminology
7039 Lindero Lane, Suite 2
Rancho Murieta, CA 95683

Justice Information Center
P.O. Box 6000
Rockville, MD 20849
1-800-851-3420 or (301) 519-5500

▓ POLYGRAPH EXAMINERS

Polygraph examiners interview and screen individuals to determine the truth or falsity of their statements. This is achieved by attaching the individual to a polygraph machine, which records their heart rate, blood pressure, respiration, and electrodermal skin resistance. A series of questions are asked and the answers noted, while the physiological responses are recorded on a moving graph. The graph is then evaluated by the polygraph examiner who interprets and diagnoses those reactions for veracity, using numerically scored charts and computer algorithms. If the results are inconclusive, another examiner will be contacted for a second opinion.

In order for a polygraph to be properly conducted, the person being examined must be willing. The examiner must have sufficient background data on both the subject and the allegations against him. The examiner should be neutral and uninfluenced by his employer (both prosecutors and defense teams engage polygraphs in their investigations). Except in extreme circumstances, the results of polygraph examinations are not admitted in court. They can be quite useful, however, in eliminating potential suspects.

Becoming a Polygraph Examiner

Qualifications

Job qualifications for polygraph examiners vary by state, but always include a combination of college education (two to five years) and practical experience (one to five years). In addition, examiners must receive specialized polygraph training at a certified technical school or college, pass the subsequent written and oral exams, and work under the supervision of a licensed polygraph examiner for six to twelve months.

Salary

The salary range of polygraph examiners is between $28,000 and $32,000 annually.

Training

Eligibility for polygraph training is based on a combination of work and education, and varies by state. Once those requirements are met, the course of study generally involves the following:

- History of the polygraph.
- Mechanics of the polygraph machine.

- Fundamental construction of test questions.
- Conducting a polygraph test.
- Analyzing polygraph charts.
- Interview and post-testing procedures.
- Ethics.
- Legal issues.
- Anatomy and physiology.
- General psychology.

This is followed by oral and written examinations and a period of supervised work. Polygraph licenses are generally not transferable as each state has different requirements.

The Courts

THE U.S. COURT SYSTEM IS DESIGNED TO SECURE AND balance the rights of the accused with the rights of society, an ideal exemplified by its symbol of a blindfolded woman holding in equal balance the scales of justice. Whether the courts achieve this goal is a topic of frequent and often vociferous debate, but that is certainly the prescribed intent.

U.S. courts are empowered under the state or federal government. States are free to create laws and statutes supplemental to those of the federal government. States can not, however, easily implement laws that contradict federal laws.

The Constitution determines whether a case is tried in state or federal court. Federal courts are traditionally empowered to try crimes against the government such as treason or violence against federal officials, and violations of civil rights such as "hate crimes" committed based on race or religious persuasion. In regard to civil cases, federal courts preside over multijurisdictional "class action" suits; cases involving one state against another; and cases brought against federal agencies. State courts are traditionally intended to handle the bulk of criminal and civil cases.

There are more than 15,000 federal and state courts operating in the United States. Both state and federal courts conduct criminal and civil trials. Criminal trials involve prosecutions for criminal activity, while civil trials involve disputes over property, compensation for accidental death or injury, or group "class-action" suits.

Arguing the Case

Prosecutors, Defense Attorneys, and Paralegals

W HETHER IT'S THE SUPREME COURT OR A SMALL-TOWN courthouse, the skill and expertise of certain participants in every trial may inspire a jury to convict a criminal or clear the name of an innocent person. Their job has inspired admiration in some and disgust in others, and has provided the basis for more than one comedian's joke. These trial participants are, of course, the lawyers. Part orator, part detective, always an advocate for the client, the trial attorney is probably the most visible and most vocal participant in the courtroom phase of any criminal or civil action.

■ COURTROOM LAWYERS

Lawyers specialize in a variety of fields, including civil, environmental, international, corporate, and, of course, criminal law. Within those specialties there are further divisions. Some attorneys focus on legal research and precedents, some are experts at arranging pleas that keep their clients' cases from going to trial, and some are trial lawyers who spend the bulk of their time preparing for and appearing in court.

Seven out of ten attorneys are in private practice. Those in public service are primarily prosecutors, although public defenders are retained through the state. Most government offices at federal, state, and local levels have staff representation, and outside attorneys may also be retained for specific suits.

In the area of criminal justice, the role of prosecutors and defense attorneys begins once the suspect is arrested. A series of steps takes the accused from arrest to trial.

1. *The Preliminary Appearance*—the judge informs suspects of the tentative charges against them and informs them of their rights, including the right to counsel. At this point the prosecutor begins to solidify her case.

2. *The Preliminary Hearing*—the prosecutor presents evidence and attempts to establish probable cause that the defendant committed the crime. At this time an indictment may be handed down officially charging the defendant.

3. *The Arraignment*—the defendant is brought into court and formally charged. The defendant then enters a plea, usually "not guilty," and makes arrangements for trial. Of course, a "guilty" or "no contest" (a non-admission of guilt, which nonetheless results in some degree of sentencing) plea waives the right to trial and the defendant goes directly from arraignment to sentencing. This is the time when bail is requested, and the defendant makes arrangements to remain free while awaiting trail or is remanded to custody.

Prosecutors

Prosecutors are employed by federal, state, and local governments. At the local level they are led by district attorneys

(DAs), generally elected to four-year terms, who oversee staff attorneys known as assistant district attorneys (ADAs) or deputy attorneys. State prosecutors' offices are headed by the attorney generals, elected in forty-three states and appointed in the rest. Their staffs comprise deputy attorney generals. At the federal level is the U.S. attorney general. Each of these officials is responsible for assigning and overseeing cases and coordinating with other branches of law enforcement and legislative offices.

Once a suspect has been arrested, and the DA has assigned the case, the ADA begins the job of prosecuting. "I'm convinced that if you step back and ask, 'Where can I do the most good?', criminal prosecution offers the best opportunity," says Mark Larson, a King County, Washington prosecuting attorney. "The array of decisions prosecutors make concerning who to charge with a crime, what precise charges should be brought, when and what negotiations should be pursued, and the like, are unique within the criminal justice system."

Those decisions are made by working closely with the police. Prosecutors visit the crime scene, review the evidence, reinterview key witnesses, request additional forensic work, and prepare for trial. Often witnesses are prepared so that the prosecution can avoid embarrassing surprises or lapses in testimony.

According to Larson, it takes human understanding and compassion to do a good job in the courtroom. "There is a lot of social psychology that's needed for this job to deal effectively with witnesses, victims, judges, and juries. Having the ability to work with all kinds of people is almost as important as having the legal skills. These are the types of skills that people can learn while working in the service industry, like waiting tables. In fact, that is a plus on a résumé as far as I am concerned."

Prosecutors have discretion, and the good ones use it, Larson says. "Most of the people I prosecute are kind of tragic. They've made a lot of bad choices, and most deserve what they get. However, it is important to strike a balance and look for a principled approach. That means that in some cases you prosecute to the fullest extent of the law. In others, you have to take the surrounding circumstances into account to find a just outcome."

Defense Attorneys

Defense attorneys are advocates for the accused, charged with reminding the jurors that in the U.S. system of justice, the defendant is "innocent until proven guilty." They review the case against the defendant, seek evidence and witnesses to corroborate the defendant's story, ensure that the evidence was properly and legally obtained, and work with forensic and other experts to develop a persuasive defense for their client.

King County Defense Attorney Theresa Olson works in the public defender's office. While preparing for law school she was involved in a near fatal accident when a drunk driver hit her. Her anger over the incident sent her to the prosecutor's office when she left law school but the job wasn't what she'd hoped for. "I interned at the office but wasn't that intrigued by the work. Then I started at the public defender's office and I really clicked with the people and loved the work."

Olson is well aware that many people don't grasp the importance of what she does. "Sometimes the criticism about my work bothers me. A lot of times I go into court and the facts are overwhelmingly against me and my client is overwhelmingly guilty. But I'm still proud of what I do."

When it's in the best interest of the client, the defense attorney may negotiate a "plea bargain" detailing mitigating circumstances or offering valuable information in exchange for a reduced charge and lesser sentence. No matter the crime, "Everybody deserves to have at least one person on their side," Olson says.

One of Olson's cases involved an older man who had worked hard all his life. But when his wife developed breast cancer, his savings were wiped out and they were forced to live in their car. In desperation, he robbed five banks. "He was guilty, no doubt about it," Olson says, "but there were mitigating circumstances. He could have gotten a very stiff sentence, but he got seventy-two months. I considered that a great victory, and I fought hard for him." Defense attorneys— particularly public defenders, who may handle twenty to thirty cases at a given time—spend a great deal of time in court, sometimes as many as three or four days per week.

Becoming a Prosecutor or Defense Attorney

In order to pass the state bar examination and become a licensed attorney, those wanting a career in law go through a rigorous education process.

Attorneys must first earn an undergraduate degree; courses useful for developing legal skills include English, public speaking, economics, and philosophy. Candidates for law school then take the Law School Admission Test (LSAT), and those scores, in addition to a good grade point average (GPA) and academic interview, determine not only whether a student is accepted to law school but the caliber of the school she will attend. The standing of the law school from which a candidate graduates can have an enormous impact on her career, both in the areas of salary and job opportunities.

The first half of law-school education is focused on fundamentals such as constitutional law, contracts, torts, civil procedure, research, and legal writing. The second half is focused on a more specialized course of study such as tax, criminal, or corporate law. During this time students may participate in school-sponsored legal clinics and gain practical experience working at legal-aid clinics, clerking for judges, or serving as interns at private law firms or government offices.

In school, students may participate in moot court, conducting mock trials under the supervision of practicing attorneys and judges. Law-school graduates receive a *juris doctor*, commonly referred to as a JD degree. The graduate may then be recruited to work at a law firm, but is not an officially licensed attorney with courtroom privileges she passes the bar exam.

Most states require practicing attorneys to participate in continuing legal education (CLE), which insures that clients receive good representation by keeping attorneys informed of new and changing legal developments, statutes, and trends.

Qualifications

Lawyers must complete undergraduate studies and receive good scores on the LSAT for law-school acceptance. To practice after graduation, they must pass the state bar examination. Licenses to practice law are not transferable from state to state, but practicing law in a different state may only require a retaking of the bar exam if the attorney is sufficiently prepared.

Salary

Starting salaries for new law-school graduates generally range from $30,000 to $50,000 annually, depending on the hiring firm and the internships and scholastic record of the graduate.

▓ PARALEGALS

Paralegals (or legal assistants) work under the direction and supervision of an attorney, providing support to defense and prosecuting attorneys. They are not permitted to charge legal fees, give legal advice, or conduct a court case. Still, there are many attorneys' duties that paralegals carry out, such as background checks, fact-finding, legal research, preparation of documents for trial, filing of legal briefs, preparation of reports, and the gathering of information for hearings. Paralegals practice in all areas of law, just as attorneys do.

Becoming a Paralegal

Qualifications

Paralegal education is available through vocational certificate programs, community and four-year colleges, and universities. The curriculum covers topics such as legal research methodology, criminal law, estate planning and probate, and family law. Paralegals must complete a certificate program (generally two years) or graduate from a community college, four-year college, or university.

Salary

Beginning salaries for paralegals range from $25,000 to $32,000 annually.

Order in the Courts
Judges and Courtroom Personnel

F OR A TRIAL TO BE PROPERLY AND FAIRLY CONDUCTED, THE RULES of law and courtroom procedure must be strictly adhered to. A defendant's outburst, a sobbing family member, or an inappropriately admitted piece of evidence could result in a mistrial, wasting the court's time and the public's money. This chapter describes the role of public servants, from judges to security, who maintain order in the court.

■ THE JUDGE

It is the duty of the judge to oversee all courtroom legal proceedings and ensure that they are conducted fairly. Judges preside over hearings and trials in all aspects of the criminal and civil justice system ranging from traffic tickets to accidental-death lawsuits to trials of premeditated murder.

During pretrial hearings the judge hears prosecution evidence, determines whether there is enough for trial, and makes some early rulings on testimony and evidence admissibility.

During a trial, the judge has a variety of duties, including determining whether potentially questionable evidence or witness testimony is allowed to be presented, ruling on objections and other motions, enforcing court protocol, and keeping the attorneys on course in their questioning.

The verdict of guilty or not guilty is generally rendered by the jury except in the case of a bench trial, when that decision is rendered by the judge. This verdict generally stands, although if the judge believes that there has been a miscarriage of justice, he or she is empowered to set aside the verdict. Once a jury renders a guilty verdict the judge imposes the sentence. In some cases defendants may waive a jury trial so the verdict and possible sentencing are both the purview of the judge.

When not in court, judges conduct research on legal issues and precedents, write opinions, and oversee administrative and clerical staff.

Becoming a Judge

Judges in federal court are appointed by the president and confirmed by the Senate. Often they are legal scholars or long-time legal practitioners. State court judges are both elected and appointed. Justices of the peace, magistrates, and county court judges work in lower courts, and are elected to preside over cases such as traffic, misdemeanors, or small-claims actions. Once elected or appointed, judges are required to take specialized state-sponsored training where they learn the particulars of their job including courtroom procedure, guidelines for admissibility of evidence, and ethics.

Qualifications

Judges are generally required to have a law degree and be a licensed attorney and a member of a bar association.

Salary

Salaries for federal court judges range between $115,000 and $133,000 annually. Salaries for state court judges range between $80,000 and $133,000 annually.

■ COURT REPORTER

The court reporter records, completely and with 100 percent accuracy, all of the activity that takes place during trial, including testimony, objections, judicial rulings, and jury instructions.

Court reporters transcribe and submit the trial record on a daily basis, allowing judges and attorneys to review what has been stated at any time during the proceedings. At the end of the trial all transcriptions are assembled and submitted as the official trial record, the invaluable basis for trial reviews or appeals.

Court reporters are not employed exclusively in the courtroom. They regularly take depositions for both prosecutors and defense attorneys in civil and criminal matters, and may also be engaged to document proceedings such as Congressional meetings.

Becoming a Court Reporter

Qualifications

Court reporters receive certification after completing a two- to four-year course of study at a vocational or technical school or college, and passing a state certification test. Not all jurisdictions require certification, however, but instead rely on a demonstration of the candidate's ability to do the job.

The National Court Reporters Association has approved more than a hundred programs that teach computer-aided transcription and use of the stenotype machine. The stenotype is a shorthand machine on which one key represents a series of letters, sounds, words, or phrases that are recorded on computer disks. Computer-aided software then transcribes the symbols.

Salary

Salaries for court reporters range from $32,000 to $40,000 annually.

■ BAILIFF

The bailiff announces the judge's arrival in the courtroom, maintains courtroom order, calls witnesses to the stand, and supervises the jury.

If the jury is sequestered, bailiffs oversee all of their activities outside the courtroom. They examine and approve reading and viewing materials, accompany visitors to and from the sequestered jurors, and generally make sure that the jurors do not discuss the trial with each other or anyone else. The bailiff also ensures that no information about the trial, aside from information presented daily in court, is available to jurors.

Bailiffs frequently are armed law enforcement officials. At the state level they may be members of the sheriff's department, and in federal court they are provided by the Marshals Service.

Becoming a Bailiff

Qualifications

Federal court bailiffs must have graduated from an accredited law enforcement academy, have three years of law enforcement experience, and complete the Department of Justice weapons proficiency test. At the state level, bailiffs generally have some police academy training and have passed a firearm proficiency test.

Salary

Salaries for federal court bailiffs range from $28,500 to $43,000 annually. Salaries for state court bailiffs range from $26,500 to $37,000 annually.

■ COURT CLERK

The court clerk is responsible for issuing jury summonses, contacting or subpoenaing witnesses, and maintaining records of criminal cases. During the course of the trial clerks swear in witnesses. Additionally, they maintain custody of all trial evidence and number and label it for identification purposes.

Becoming a Court Clerk

Qualifications

Court clerk jobs require basic clerical and computer skills, good organizational ability and follow-through, and a willingness to learn and work in a structured environment. Most court clerks possess a bachelor's degree, usually in business administration. Often they receive on-the-job training.

Salary

Salaries for court clerks range from $27,000 to $34,000 annually.

Corrections
From Prison to Parole

T HE PRISON POPULATION OF THE UNITED STATES IS THE largest in the world, in part due to an explosion of stiffer sentencing laws, such as "three strikes" (which requires a mandatory life sentence for anyone convicted of three felonies, regardless of their severity); the war on drugs; and increasingly hard-line public officials. The prison population has greatly increased in recent years and consequently, so has the number of newly constructed prisons.

The bottom line is that there is a lot of work available in the field of corrections.

In some small towns and rural areas the prison has become the primary employer, replacing agricultural and other industries. In California, which under former governor Pete Wilson experienced an explosion of prison construction, correctional officers have achieved enormous political clout through sheer numbers and political contributions.

The focus increasingly seems to be moving away from rehabilitation. In Texas, for example, Governor George W. Bush began his tenure by dismantling the Texas Correctional Institutions' drug treatment program, which under former governor Ann Richards was the most comprehensive in the nation. However, there is still some good being done in prisons. Every day experts in drug treatment, training and education, and psychological rehabilitation work to help prisoners become more useful and productive citizens once they leave prison.

Prisons are also trying some innovative programs for female inmates, enabling them to keep newborns in the prison nurseries so that mother and child can bond. This improves the child's physical and emotional health, and allows the mother to develop parenting skills and a relationship with the child that may help both to have a better future.

The private sector is also getting involved in prisons. Some are able to hire convicts to work for privately owned companies. The person taking a phone order for services or merchandise may very well be incarcerated while doing so. Others use prisoners for manufacturing, creating concerns among competitors who have to pay market wages for labor.

While controversial, these programs offer some benefits to the prisoners, who learn job skills and, perhaps for the first time in their lives, the discipline and rewards of working an eight-hour day.

People who work in corrections must find ways to balance society's needs with those of prisoners, and ensure that the prisoner pays for their crime while not creating an environment that will make them more likely to offend once they leave. Discipline, compassion, and resourcefulness are qualities needed for those considering work in the growing and changing field of corrections.

CHAPTER TWELVE

Working in the Prison System
Correctional Officers, Wardens, and Correctional Treatment Specialists

A CCORDING TO A 1999 ARTICLE IN THE CHICAGO TRIBUNE, the prison population in the United States has more than doubled in recent years. This rapid growth is attributable largely to drug prosecutions, and additionally to increasing intolerance for crime reflected in longer prison sentences and "truth in sentencing" laws, which require convicts to serve the bulk of their sentences rather than receive early parole. Two-thirds of incarcerated persons are in state or federal prison, and the other third in municipal or county jail.

Maintaining order in these facilities is the job of correctional officers. The National Institute of Corrections reports that more than 180,000 correctional officers are employed by state and federal prisons.

■ CORRECTIONAL OFFICERS

The primary duties of the correctional officer are to maintain order and security, observe and record prisoner behavior, enforce rules and regulations, and prevent disturbances in the jails, reformatories, and penitentiaries in which they serve. Correctional officers must also prevent prison escapes. Additionally, they are sometimes contracted to work in county jails, which are primarily staffed by the sheriff's department.

There are distinctions between jails and prisons and the populations that inhabit them. The job of correctional officers in each facility varies accordingly.

Jails generally have a transient population. People remanded to jail are usually serving short sentences for lesser crimes such as disturbing the peace, drunk and disorderly conduct, or other misdemeanors. They may be incarcerated in jail while awaiting trial because the defendant is unable to afford bail or because the charge is so serious that bail has been denied. According to the Bureau of Labor Statistics, more than twenty-two million people are processed through the jail system every year, and more than half a million are in jail at any given time.

It is rare for correctional officers to be employed in county jails, but when they are their sole responsibility is to guard the prisoners.

Prison populations are generally more constant. These inmates generally serve longer sentences than those in jail, and the population contains more violent offenders. (Facilities geared toward "white collar" crime are the exception.)

Correctional officers in state and federal prisons have an expansive list of duties, including:

- Monitoring the daily activities of prisoners including work, exercise, and meals.
- Searching cells for weapons, drugs, fire hazards, or other contraband.
- Inspecting locks, doors, and windows for signs of tampering.

- Intervening and employing physical control during fights, riots, or attempted escapes.
- Writing reports detailing the prisoners' behavior, such as the quality of their work assignments or involvement in disturbances.
- Escorting prisoners to and from cells to meet with visitors, go to medical treatment facilities, and attend hearings or courthouse procedures.
- Maintaining order, including settling disputes between prisoners.
- Assisting law enforcement officers when crimes are committed in the institution or on the grounds.

Correctional officers are stationed inside the facility at stations ranging from the visitor's entry to cell-block patrol, or outside in towers that oversee buildings, yards, grounds, and walls. Correctional officers assigned to high-security areas observe the prisoners' activities via closed-circuit television at a central command post. The facility's most dangerous prisoners, from death row inmates to those determined to be too violent or erratic to mix with the general population, are housed in high-security areas. Under constant observation and supervision, these inmates can be easily tracked by computer should something go wrong.

Becoming a State Correctional Officer

Qualifications

The basic qualifications for a state correctional officer include:

- U.S. citizen.
- Between the ages of twenty-one and thirty-five.
- High-school diploma or its equivalent.

- No felony convictions.
- Pass a physical fitness assessment.
- Pass a background check.

Salary

The salaries for state correctional officers range from $26,000 to $32,000 annually.

Training

According to the National Institute of Corrections, officers receive an average of 225 hours of training, although the requirements in each state range from 0 to 400 hours. Two-thirds of those employed in corrections are men. Seventy-five percent of states require officer candidates to pass a medical exam and 65 percent use psychological screening. Just 27.6 percent of corrections officers belong to a minority group.

In a standard correctional officer course, training includes:

- Administration and personnel.
- Ethics and professionalism.
- Inmate management (including supervision, under-standing techniques of manipulation, and discipline).
- Legal issues.
- Communication.
- Officer safety.
- Applied skills (including searches and contraband, trans-portation, restraints, court procedure, security, custody, and control).
- Conflict and crisis management.
- Medical and mental health.

Becoming a Federal Correctional Officer

Qualifications

To qualify to be a federal correctional officer you must:

- Have a bachelor's degree in any field of study, three years of general work experience, or a combination of undergraduate education and qualifying work experience equaling three years.
- Submit to and pass a background check including inquiries about criminal records and character references.
- Pass a physical test.
- Pass a drug screen.

Salary

The salaries for federal correctional officers range from $26,000 to $34,000 annually.

Training

Federal correctional officers receive at least 200 hours of instructional training during their first year of employment. After their initial hire, officers complete 120 hours of specialized correctional training at the Federal Bureau of Prisons residential training center. The training covers four basic categories: firearms, self-defense, written test, and physical abilities test. Once this course is successfully completed, an additional eighty hours of training is taken in-house as on-the-job training at the assigned correctional institution. That training includes institutional policies and regulations, custody and security procedures, and diversity awareness.

To apply for a position with the Federal Bureau of Prisons, contact the nearest regional office.

▓ PRISON WARDEN

Wardens oversee and are ultimately responsible for all prison activities in addition to the preparation of and adherence to budgets and the development of prison policy. Wardens do not generally interact with prisoners on a daily basis.

Becoming a Prison Warden

Qualifications

Among the important characteristics for those seeking employment as a prison warden are:

- Good planner.
- Good communicator.
- Willing to lead.
- Fiscal skills.
- High ethics, values, and integrity.
- Goal-oriented.
- Flexibility.

Salary

The salaries for prison wardens range from $45,000 to $62,000 annually.

Training

Wardens traditionally work their way through the correctional ranks to attain this highest possible supervisory position. The National Institute of Corrections Academy, a division of the National Institute of Corrections, has established training curricula for prison wardens. Although the National Institute of Corrections is a federal agency, it works with various state departments of corrections to establish national standards for prison warden training. The Department of Corrections has established training curricula, which consist of four levels geared toward developing leadership skills for those on the supervisory career track. That curriculum progresses as follows:

Level one (mandatory for all supervisors). This basic supervisory course or its equivalent must be completed within one year of any promotion.

Level two. The candidate must earn a bachelor's degree or complete 100 hours of documented management training.

Level three. The candidate must earn a master's degree in management or administration, or complete fifty hours of documented management training.

Level four. Additional programs and requirements are designated and assigned by the corrections academy director.

Supervisors and wardens must also receive a minimum of forty hours of documented training annually to keep their job certificates.

■ CORRECTIONAL TREATMENT SPECIALISTS

Most prison inmates will eventually be released into society. Correctional treatment specialists attempt to make the inmate's reentry as smooth as possible. As case managers, they evaluate the progress of inmates, establish training programs, provide case reports to the parole commission, and work with the prisoners and their families to develop plans for release and parole. They analyze the needs of the prison's inmates and provide an environment in which inmates can develop skills and prepare for a clean life after prison.

Training for treatment jobs varies by specialty. Those seeking work in these fields should consider an undergraduate degree in psychology or social work. Post-undergraduate studies could include graduate studies in psychology or education and supervised clinical work in both community and correctional settings.

Qualifying for a corrections position is a somewhat inexact science. Determining how an individual's specific education and employment history pertains to a given corrections position is best done by visiting or corresponding with the human resources or hiring division of the law enforcement or social services division in the desired agency.

Becoming a Corrections Specialist

Corrections specialists maintain the library for the department of corrections. They aid prison workers by researching and compiling information on trends in corrections. Patricia Sholes, specialist for the National Institute of Corrections in Denver, explains, "Our library is unique in that our information comes from those who work in the field and the information is focused on corrections. Our library is used primarily by those in the profession for statistics, trends, and facts." According to Patricia Sholes, "Most corrections specialists have been corrections practitioners, which gives us the background to work in this capacity."

Qualifications

The qualifications for a corrections specialist include:

- Bachelor's degree with at least twenty-four hours of social science.
- One year of professional social work experience or graduate education.

Salary

Salaries for corrections specialists range from $26,000 to $35,000 annually.

Becoming a Drug Treatment Specialist

Drug treatment specialists work with prisoners who have substance-abuse problems. They conduct drug education classes, provide counseling, develop treatment plans, and follow up on after-care plans once the inmate is released.

Qualifications

The qualifications for a drug treatment specialist include:

- Bachelor's degree in one of the behavioral sciences.
- An undergraduate course that includes at least three semester hours in alcohol or drug abuse or fifty hours of actual training in alcohol and drug abuse.
- Six months of professional counseling in drug or alcohol abuse.

Salary

Salaries for drug treatment specialists range from $32,000 to $39,000 annually.

Becoming an Education Specialist

Education specialists develop the education programs in correctional institutions, including adult education and college credit programs.

Qualifications

A bachelor's degree, advanced education studies, hands-on instructional experience, and direct involvement with inmate education programs are all qualifying factors for those considering this career.

Salary

Salaries for education specialists range from $25,000 to $29,000 annually.

Working on the Streets
Parole and Probation Officers

W HEN CRIMINALS ARE RELEASED BEFORE COMPLETING THEIR
court-designated sentences, they will receive either
probation or parole. Parole is a function of the corrections
system that involves releasing the prisoner based on promise
and likelihood of good behavior. Probation involves the sus-
pension of a jail sentence so that the convicted person is not
incarcerated but still under the supervision of the court.

The people involved in the oversight of those on release are
known as probation and parole officers. They enforce the rules
of release, keep track of those under their supervision, monitor their employment and living situations, and react to violations of the conditional release—often by taking the offender
back into custody. These officers protect society while offering
a second chance to those who have broken the law.

■ TRAINING

Training qualifications for these positions vary greatly by
state. Below are two examples of state requirements. Contact

your state's qualifying agency to ensure that you are pursuing the correct course of study.

Nevada Division of Parole and Probation

Job candidates must complete the standard post police officer training with 480 hours of division-specific training including classes on the criminal justice system, Nevada's revised statutes, ethics, time management, program referrals, and substance abuse. Additional advanced training is encouraged including management, DEA narcotics investigation, gang seminars, and AIDS information.

Ohio Department of Rehabilitation and Correction

Minimum requirements are either a bachelor's degree in criminal justice, law enforcement, social service, communications, or a related field; or two years of training or experience in the probation or parole fields such as report writing, treatment referrals, case services delivery, and contact with other criminal justice agencies. Candidates must have no legal prohibition against carrying firearms and possess a valid Ohio driver's license.

Candidates meeting these qualifications must complete an assessment, which includes an interview, writing test, background investigation, and drug test. When that is successfully completed, the candidate must attend three weeks of training at the corrections training academy and, within one year of hire, become certified in unarmed self-defense by the adult parole authority, with recertification required annually.

■ PAROLE OFFICERS

Parole officers work with the correctional system. Once the prisoner has been interviewed by the parole board, deemed a good risk, and released from incarceration, the parole office is his first destination.

The first duty of a parole officer is to assess the level of supervision required by her new client. This assessment generally falls into one of four categories:

1. *High-control*—parolees require strict supervision. They have generally been convicted of a violent offense and have a high risk of repeating the behavior.
2. *High-service*—parolees need extra support securing psychological, physical, or employment help.
3. *Control and service*—parolees require both moderate supervision and support to begin their new lives.
4. *Minimum*—parolees require only the legal minimum of supervision and assistance.

In order to assist their clients in successfully reentering society, parole officers work closely with service agencies such as employment referral offices, drug treatment centers, medical and mental health clinics, and other community services.

Parole officers set the conditions (or terms) of parole, which generally include:

- No criminal conduct.
- Steady employment.
- Attendance at scheduled parole meetings.
- Notification of change of address.
- No ingestion or possession of drugs, alcohol, or contraband of any kind.
- No association with known felons.
- No use or possession of weapons.

Any violations of these conditions may (and generally do) result in the parolee being returned to prison.

Parole officers oversee a variety of prisoner release programs. They include:

1. *Reentry programs*—parolees are placed in halfway houses or other less restrictive surroundings before making the transition into living on their own.
2. *Work furlough*—inmates are released from prison during the day to work and return to incarceration at night and on weekends for an interim period precluding full parole.
3. *House arrest*—low-risk prisoners are confined to their homes for the duration of their sentence. These prisoners wear electronic monitoring devices that allow them to leave their homes within prescribed parameters of time and distance in order to work.

Becoming a Parole Officer

Qualifications

To become a parole officer, the following requirements must be met:

- Bachelor's degree (preferably in criminal justice, social work, psychology, or a related behavioral science).
- Strong interpersonal skills.
- Ability to elicit cooperation and command authority.

Salary

Parole officers can expect starting salaries between $24,000 and $33,000 annually.

▓ PROBATION OFFICERS

Probation takes place when a person is convicted but the judge determines that confinement is not warranted. Instead, that person is placed on probation and is allowed to live in society but under the court's supervision. Terms of probation often include psychological or chemical-dependency treatment and mandatory community service. People who receive probation are generally considered low risk and the goal of probation officers is to involve them in community service and steer them away from criminal behavior.

Between 30 and 60 percent of convicted offenders are sentenced to some form of probation. Probation officers supervise their activities, make court recommendations after conducting an assessment, interview those being considered for probation to determine their plans upon release, refer them to community programs, and visit them in both their home and work environments.

Unlike parole, in probation the judge sets the terms of release. Those terms are generally that the probationer must:

- Remain law abiding.
- Maintain a job.
- Remain within the jurisdictional boundaries of the presiding court.
- Neither possess nor use firearms.
- Not associate with known felons.
- Meet restrictions tailored to the individual offense such as drug or alcohol treatment, anger management, parenting instruction, or financial restitution to the crime victim or a charitable or community organization.

Probation officers may also be involved in alternative sentencing programs. In "boot camp" programs the offender goes to a military-style camp whose regimen involves physical training, strict discipline, and hard labor. In "scared straight" programs, youth offenders visit prisons, and inmates talk about their lives and the reality of day-to-day incarceration.

Some communities around the country have stationed probation officers in schools to supervise and guide the progress of juvenile offenders who are still attending classes. The goal of these programs is to maintain a constant presence that focuses on troubled or "at-risk" students and ensures safety within the school. In light of recent school shootings, these officers can be seen as particularly important due to their ability to detect early warning signs in students who have a potential for violence and intervene with the help they need.

Becoming a Probation Officer for Adult Defenders

Qualifications

Parole officers for adults must meet the following requirements:

- Bachelor's degree in criminal justice, social work, psychology, or a related field.
- Two years of experience as a counselor.
- Ability to work effectively with people who may be hostile and uncooperative.
- Strong interpersonal skills.

Salary

Probation officers earn starting salaries between $24,000 and $32,000 annually.

Becoming a Probation Officer for Juvenile Offenders

Juvenile probation officers also work through the court system and are responsible for supervising and helping juvenile offenders (eighteen years of age or younger) who have been placed on probation.

These specialists work closely with the courts, offenders, and their families. They conduct assessments that may include determining the offender's treatment needs, history of family interaction (and possible abuse), and school and social schedule and activities, and recommending participation in supervised diversionary programs.

Their goal is to steer juvenile offenders away from criminal activity through community programs and activities. The families of these juveniles are also referred to programs and agencies. Family participation is vital because statistics show the home environment is a major influence on whether a juvenile returns to delinquent behavior.

Qualifications

Juvenile probation officers must meet the following requirements:

- Bachelor's degree in criminal justice, social work, psychology, or a related field.
- Two years of experience as a counselor.
- Ability to handle large caseloads.
- Ability to effectively communicate with juveniles who may be hostile.

Salary

Juvenile probation officers may expect to begin at salaries between $24,000 and $32,000 annually.

Private Security

Whether it's tracking a wayward husband to a nearby motel, protecting celebrities from overly familiar fans at a popular restaurant, or watching over merchandise at the local mall, private security seems to be everywhere these days.

Americans are extraordinarily safety-conscious. Gated communities, home security, classroom instruction on "stranger danger," and self-defense classes are all signs of the national mania for safety. In addition, the United States is the most heavily armed nation in the world; every law-abiding citizen has the right to keep arms on their property to protect their home.

Inside corporate America there are also fears that employees may be stealing anything from reams of paper to software secrets. This type of crime is not on the top of public law enforcement's priority list, so private security often picks up the slack, conducting in-house investigations that may save employers millions of dollars. Insurance companies estimate that theft may be responsible for one-third of business failures, resulting in lost jobs, opportunity, and revenue.

CHAPTER FOURTEEN

Guarding People and Property
Security Officers, Bodyguards, and Security Managers

WHETHER IT'S A SECURITY GUARD SAFELY ESCORTING A LATE night shopper to her car in a deserted parking garage or a burly bodyguard escorting a pop star safely past his screaming fans, security professionals are in the business of making individuals feel safe. Overseeing them are security managers who ensure that the guards are in the right place at the right time to keep the client from harm.

■ SECURITY OFFICERS

The most visible members of the private security field are security officers, also known as security guards. They are stationed at department stores and entertainment complexes, banks and office buildings, airports and hospitals, federal buildings, and nuclear power plants. Most do their job on their feet, either by walking an assigned area or monitoring screens linked to security cameras. Some security guards work vehicle patrols in parking garages or residential communities to watch for signs of trouble or respond to emergency calls.

A variety of duties may be part of the security guard's job, including:

- Inspecting and patrolling property for unsecured doors and windows, safety and fire hazards, security violations, mechanical or maintenance problems, and trespass by unauthorized persons.
- Maintaining ongoing oversight, either through their physical presence or security monitors and other safety devices.
- Monitoring visitors by checking identification, issuing visitor passes or badges, and maintaining a sign-in log of those entering and exiting a building or facility. This duty is also performed by security-gate guards charged with monitoring those entering and exiting large areas of private property.

Security guards may interact and work with law enforcement officers at major events such as concerts or street fairs. Their role at such events is to assist in controlling crowds, intervene in any disturbances, and monitor and control drug use and underage drinking.

Private security is also used in the nation's courts in addition to and under supervision of sheriffs' deputies.

Becoming a Security Officer

Retired law enforcement officer Ron Edwards now works as a supervisor for United International Investigative Services (UIIS), a multiservice private security firm. UIIS contracts with companies, federal courts, prisons, embassies, and consulates in both the United States and abroad. One of their contracts is a federal courthouse. "Our basic job is to protect the court family. We have to deal with people who are in the courthouse for a lot of different reasons." Which is why, Edwards says, he prefers to hire former police officers. "They have insight and the ability to profile people in a short amount of time—usually just the moments required to pass through the metal detector—and act on suspicious behavior. A lot of what we do in private security is to prevent a crime from happening in the first place."

Court security officers are stationed at the building entrances where they run the X ray detecting machine. "During the screening process we've detected all kinds of weapons that we had to confiscate and turn over to local police," Edwards says.

The job of a court security officer is not always routine. In one incident a pipe bomb was discovered outside the courthouse building. "We had to secure the building and provide security until the police department came in and disarmed the bomb," Edwards says. "In another incident we actually had an explosive device go off in front of the building. Thankfully no one was hurt." Though they do happen, these occurrences are not regular. "What we usually have is a lot of minor situations," Edwards says. "Like the time we had an attorney who got unruly in court and then got into a physical confrontation with law enforcement officers."

Qualifications

Most states require private security officers to obtain licenses. The general qualifications include:

- At least eighteen years old.
- Pass a background check.
- Complete security-officer training on topics such as detaining people and emergency procedures.
- For those who carry firearms, pass a firearm proficiency and licensing test (for unarmed security officers, qualifications may be less stringent).

Salary

Entry-level private security positions range from $10,300 to $25,000 ($17,000 to $23,000 for federal employees) annually, with an average starting salary of $17,300, depending upon factors such as type of work, employer, and location. However, highly trained guards in charge of sensitive materials can earn as much as $35,000 annually.

Training

Individual employers usually provide preliminary and then on-the-job training for new security officers. Training includes:

- Protection.
- Techniques for detainment.
- First aid.
- Crisis intervention.
- Firearms training (for armed employees).

Employers look for traits such as the ability to maintain composure in stressful situations, good physical stamina, solid interpersonal skills, the ability to interact easily with different cultures, and good oral and written communication skills. Guards may be required to pass a polygraph and a drug screen.

Guards working in heavy security may receive additional training from a security firm or training service.

Security guards working for the federal government must meet specific criteria that include:

- Previous work experience as a security guard.
- Qualifying for the use of firearms.
- Passing a written examination.

■ CAMPUS SECURITY OFFICERS

Any parent who has sent a child to live away from home for the first time can relate to the importance of campus security. These officers have the special role of looking after a large group of young people, many of whom are experiencing freedom and life on their own for the first time.

Typically, campus security officers have the following assignments:

- Patrol a designated area, either by car or foot.
- Enforce rules and regulations specific to the college or university, in addition to federal and state laws and statutes.
- Assist city or county police and state patrol officers in case of emergency.
- Maintain surveillance of areas suspected of criminal activity.
- Investigate accidents or crimes including gathering evidence, locating witnesses to a crime or disturbance, and testifying in court.
- Issue citations for violations.

- Inspect school buildings, dormitories, and campus grounds for prowlers or vagrants, break-ins, fire and property damage, and safety violations.
- Answer telephone inquiries, monitor alarm systems, prepare reports, and operate communication equipment.
- Administer first aid.
- Direct and regulate traffic.

Becoming a Campus Security Officer

David Modena, manager of Shoreline Community College in Washington State, notes that the market for campus security jobs is growing and that people who work in the field find it satisfying and are able to earn a comfortable income.

"Our agents are officers of the college. The characteristics I look for before hiring someone are maturity, the ability to solve problems, good communication skills, and an ability to be self-directed because they spend a lot of time working alone." According to Modena, the position attracts a variety of people. "Some want to go into law enforcement and use security as a stepping stone, while others like the freedom and independence of security work. Surprisingly, there isn't a lot of turnover of campus security officers."

Another potential benefit of working on campus is education. Some facilities provide free education for officers and their spouses as part of the benefits package.

Qualifications

The minimum qualifications for a campus security position include:

- High-school diploma or equivalent.
- Two years of full-time college majoring in police science or a related field, or two years of police experience.
- Pass a written examination with oral components, a physical assessment, and a safe-driving test.
- Driver's license.

Salary

Salaries for campus security officers range from $19,000 to $24,700 annually.

Training

Police academies in most states provide training for campus security officers. These courses cover:

- Self-defense tactics.
- Review of laws and rules for arrest.
- Investigative techniques.
- Surveillance.
- Traffic control.
- Ethics.
- Report writing.

▪ EXECUTIVE PROTECTION AGENTS (BODYGUARDS)

The stereotype of the "all brawn and no brains" bodyguard is long gone, because nothing could be further from the truth. The term is even becoming obsolete. Many of these security personnel now go by the title "executive protection agents."

These safety specialists don't rely on sheer strength alone to protect their clients; they use their intelligence, experience, and training to keep them from harm.

In the movie *The Bodyguard,* Kevin Costner plays a retired Secret Service agent hired to protect and create a safe environment for a superstar who has become the target of death threats. His character's background is true-to-life. The most sought-after protection agents, particularly for high-profile executives or celebrities, are retired law enforcement officers or military personnel extensively trained in protection.

When a bodyguard is hired, the first responsibility is to conduct a threat assessment, which evaluates the weaknesses or loopholes in the new client's existing security precautions, or start from scratch to consider an entirely new security strategy. Once the assessment is complete, the agent makes a report to his supervisor, options are devised for the client's consideration, and a proposal is presented to her.

The services provided by bodyguards include:

Visible protection. This is when the protective agent attempts to be visible so that his presence deters contact with the client. This style of protection is useful in celebrity situations, for example, where the client's primary goal is to be left alone and the average fan would be intimidated by a bodyguard's presence.

Invisible protection. This is desirable at private events or public speeches where the goal is not solitude but safety. Agents dress appropriately (black tie at an awards dinner or embassy function, for example) and keep their client safe while keeping a reasonable distance.

Travel security. This involves escorting the client on national and international trips and may include chauffeur duties and hotel-room checks. If the client is traveling by private aircraft, the protection agent may check out flight personnel, do a preflight plane check, or serve as pilot. Aviation experience is a highly desirable attribute in a bodyguard.

Asset courier. This service involves transporting valuables safely from one location to another.

Rescue operations. This is a highly specialized service generally provided by guards with elite military backgrounds. They respond to hostage and kidnap situations, often in foreign countries, where domestic and foreign officials have been unsuccessful. These agents may also specialize in child retrieval in parental kidnap situations.

Battered spouse protection. This involves keeping women safe from abusive spouses. The service ranges from round-the-clock protection to escorts to and from the courthouse for divorce, custody, and other proceedings. Women unable to afford protection may be able to find bodyguards willing to provide *pro bono* protection.

Becoming an Executive Protection Agent

Discretion is a vital part of the bodyguard's job. Celebrity and other clients must be sure that the details and secrets of their private lives remain private once the assignment is finished.

Qualifications

Job qualifications vary by assignment, but in general bodyguards need a law enforcement or military background and extensive training.

Salary

Working as a bodyguard can be a lucrative assignment. Base pay averages $50,000 annually (and may go much higher), and perks include benefits of the client's lifestyle such as expensive restaurant meals, posh hotels, and first-class travel.

Training

The best training for anyone looking for a career as a bodyguard is that received by state and federal law enforcement officers and members of the military. Persons with these backgrounds may also seek private instruction in anything from foreign languages to aviation.

Executive protection agencies are growing, providing opportunities for those who want to pursue a career in protection but do not have the appropriate background. Here they'll learn weapons and martial-arts skills, site evaluation, surveillance, defensive tactics, and evasive driving. Fees and entrance qualifications vary by institution. (Check the Web sites of the professional organizations in the appendixes for sample listings.)

■ SECURITY MANAGERS

Whether employed directly by a private corporation or through an agency, security managers are a vital component in the security field. Their responsibilities include:

- Supervision of the security staff.
- Assisting in business and budget planning.
- Managing staff recruitment, selection, orientation, and training.

Becoming a Security Manager

Security managers generally need a minimum of five years of experience in the security industry or criminal justice field. A good candidate has a well-rounded understanding of security operations and human resource responsibilities; provides solid leadership, organization and planning; and can communicate clearly and effectively. Security managers must match security personnel with assignments, which may have as much to do with personality as skills. An ability to link the right person with the right job or client is vital.

Qualifications

Minimum qualifications for a security manager typically include:

- Two years of college education (preferably in criminal justice).
- Five years of work experience, or a combination of experience and education.
- Supervisory experience.
- Business management experience.
- Strong oral and written communication skills.

Salary

Depending on the size and specialties of the company or agency, security managers can expect to earn salaries from $30,000 to $60,000 annually.

The Trackers
Private Investigators and Bounty Hunters

A N ELDERLY WOMAN SEEKS HER LONG LOST BROTHER. AN ANGRY
bail bondsman needs a missing felon at his court date
so the bail isn't forfeited. When a person is missing or information must be found, professional investigators and bounty
hunters are ready for the job.

▓ PRIVATE INVESTIGATORS

The classic private investigator (PI) has his feet on his desk
and a bottle in his drawer, waiting for a beautiful but shady
blonde to come in and get him started on the case of a life-
time. Real life is a lot less "noir" and a lot more work. Private
detectives take on a broad range of criminal and civil cases.
They work for corporations, individuals, private attorneys,
and public defenders.

Private detectives use a variety of methods to do their job.
They interview witnesses, review records and other documents, conduct background checks, and maintain surveillance. Much like a police stakeout, detectives monitor their

subjects for long periods of time and document their findings with video or still photography. The Internet has been a boon for detectives who use it to investigate background information, hidden assets, missing persons, and details about professions, businesses, and locations that may be vital to the case.

Types of Investigations

Detectives specialize or perform a broad range of investigations. The following is a partial list of some common investigations.

Legal Investigations

Detectives who perform legal investigations are involved in the criminal justice system. Often employed by criminal defense attorneys, legal investigation detectives attempt to counter the prosecution's case by conducting their own investigation. They seek new witnesses, track down those who have disappeared, and interview the prosecution's witnesses regarding their testimony. Detectives look for new evidence, taking video and photographs as appropriate, and may attempt to find alternative suspects for the crime. At trial, detectives aid the attorney in organizing and presenting the evidence, and testify in court.

Financial Investigations

Financial investigations are conducted for banks and large corporations and involve tracing assets and searching for evidence of embezzlement or fraud. These cases include tracking down a partner or employee who has disappeared with funds. These investigators must be computer experts as most fund transfers, stock, and other transactions are done not with hard currency but electronically.

Corporate Investigations

Corporate investigations generally focus on theft of both physical and intellectual property. The software industry is a hotbed of intellectual-property theft, where new ideas for everything from Web search engines to video games are closely guarded. Investigators for corporations may also conduct employee background checks. This can be done on-line through databases, or—if the situation warrants—may require a more hands-on approach including checking court records and talking to neighbors.

Marital Infidelity and Premarital Investigations

Marital infidelity and premarital investigations are the cheater's worst nightmare. These detectives use surveillance, video, and occasionally live decoys to give an unhappy spouse the proof they need, even if it's not information they really want to see. Increasingly, doubting fiancées are hiring detectives to make sure they're not about to make the biggest mistake of their lives. Decoys are used to see if the fiancé can be lured into infidelity. Evidence collected by investigators allows the spouse or fiancée to confront their partner with hard facts rather than suspicion.

Background Investigations

Background investigations are conducted on corporate employees, and increasingly on domestic ones as well. A spate of allegations about abusive child-care workers has prompted worried parents to stop relying on domestic agencies and to check nannies and domestic workers themselves. In addition to a thorough background investigation, detectives may set up a hidden home-surveillance camera so that parents have video evidence regarding their child. Premarital background checks are also conducted to reveal a criminal past or financial difficulties.

Harassment Investigations

Harassment investigations may involve an angry ex-lover or unknown stalker. Through surveillance, phone monitoring, and witness interviews, detectives can establish the identity of an unknown harasser or compile enough evidence to assist the victim in obtaining a restraining order.

A private detective must be self-motivated and independent. They should have a good rapport with people and a keen perception of their surroundings. The nature of the work makes regular encounters of a hostile nature a fact of life, so the ability to remain calm even when provoked is imperative. Long and irregular hours and occasionally dangerous situations come with the territory.

Becoming a Private Investigator

Qualifications

In most states, private investigators must be licensed. The usual requirements to receive a license include:

- At least eighteen years old.
- Citizen or resident alien of the United States.
- No felony convictions.
- Pay all required fees.
- Submit fingerprints for file records.
- Obtain required permit and training to carry firearms.

Salary

Compensation varies widely, but detectives generally bill $50 to $150 per hour plus expenses.

Training

No formal education is mandated by states, but most private investigators have a high-school diploma and many have at least some college or a bachelor's degree.

Employers, however, do have requirements. For instance, a detective wishing to work on criminal cases would need either a law enforcement background or extensive training in evidence collection and criminal procedures. Excellent computer skills or a background in finance could also open the door to detective work in these areas.

Classes are available for those interested in careers in private detecting. Additionally, books are available concerning how to track down loved ones, assets, or background information.

■ BOUNTY HUNTERS

The lone stranger or determined posse out to get the wanted culprit "dead or alive"—and the reward that comes with it—is a staple of American lore. The truth is that little has changed since the days of the Old West. Reaction to recent deadly mistakes by overzealous bounty hunters may finally result in much-needed laws and restrictions. But currently they operate almost without restriction and can use any technique including abduction and breaking and entering to get their target, known in the trade as a "skip."

Mackenzie Green, considered by many to be the best bounty hunter in the business, depends on her gut instincts and way with the people to capture the skip using a combination of tracking skills and a chameleonlike ability to fit in anywhere. By the time the subject of her pursuit figures out who she is, she has them in custody.

Bounty hunters are contracted by bail bondsmen, whose business is to loan bail money to criminal defendants in exchange for a fee and a promise that they will appear in court until the case is complete and the bondsmen's cash is returned. Failure to show up results in bail forfeiture and the bondsman has a limited window of time to find and return the skip before the forfeiture is final. This is where the bounty hunter comes in.

The bounty hunter tracks the skip and then brings him or her back to court custody. For this service they may receive as much as 50 percent of the forfeited bond and the bondsman is able to cut the loss in half.

Becoming a Bounty Hunter

Not all states permit bounty hunters to carry guns so street smarts and common sense are the primary tools of a good bounty hunter. Bounty hunters try to avoid grabbing the skip in public places; innocent citizens could get hurt in the process and well-meaning citizens might believe they're witnessing a kidnapping and intervene. The bounty hunter's greatest asset is the element of surprise, so it's important to grab the suspect on the first attempt because there may not be another opportunity.

Bail is regulated by the insurance code, penal code, administrative code, and local ordinances, and the state insurance department licenses bail bondsmen. In some states, bondsmen must attend a certified two-day class to be licensed. They are restricted from colluding with lawyers, newspapers, or court officials to gain business. Oddly, bondsmen are held to stricter standards and oversight than the bounty hunters they hire.

Bounty hunters are empowered to:

- Hold a defendant captive until trial.
- Arrest, transport, and surrender a skip to court without warrants or other legal authority.
- Use force at their own discretion when capturing a fugitive.
- Forcibly abduct a skip to return them to court custody.

Concerns are increasing about these powers. Incidents involving the injury and destruction of property belonging to innocent persons have spurred some states to enact licensing and training laws and other restrictions on bounty hunters. Illinois, Kentucky, and Oregon have outlawed private bounty hunters.

Qualifications

Restrictions are being enacted on a state-by-state basis. Contact your local law enforcement agency for details in your area.

Salary

Depending upon the forfeited bail, bounty hunters can earn between $1,000 and $100,000 per assignment.

Training

There are no minimum or standardized requirements. However, those interested in this career are advised to take classes in self-defense, computer skills, and investigative techniques. Videos and books detailing the specifics of a career in bounty hunting are widely available on the Web.

Professional Organizations for Careers in Criminal Justice

A FTER DETERMINING WHICH CAREER IN CRIMINAL JUSTICE TO pursue, participating in professional organizations can help to build your career.

For persons not fully employed in their field of choice, professional organizations can be a valuable resource. Many organizations accept student or associate members, and offering to volunteer for a fund-raising event or clerical duties may help get a foot in the door.

Most of those involved in professional organizations spend the time because they want to advance not only their own careers but also the profession as a whole. They're informed and passionate and ready to assist or even mentor a newcomer who shares their vision of the possibilities inherent in their field of choice.

■ THE FRONT LINES

The International Association of Chiefs of Police (IACP) is the oldest membership organization of police executives.

Formed in 1893, it boasts more than 16,000 members in the United States and more than 100 members worldwide, representing state, local, federal, and international agencies.

The IACP provides courses on topics such as national use of fingerprint identification, homicidal tendencies, youth violence, and others that impact the law enforcement profession. The organization provides information on topics ranging from highway safety to computer technology. For more information contact:

International Association of Chiefs of Police
515 North Washington Street
Alexandria, VA 22314
1-800-THE-IACP, ext. 209

The National Center for Women and Policing was created to provide opportunities for women in policing. The center sponsors a number of national and regional conferences. Center director Penny Harrington says the organization includes members from federal, state, and local branches of law enforcement; police trainers and consultants; civilian women in policing; and community leaders, public officials, and educators.

The Center also offers development programs that provide leadership training for women in policing. Additionally, it conducts research and reports on how women perform in law enforcement, obstacles faced by women in the job, and strategies to deal with problems unique to women in the field. For more information contact:

National Center for Women and Policing
8105 West 3rd Street, Suite 1
Los Angeles, CA 90048
(323) 651-0495

The National Organization of Black Law Enforcement Officials (NOBLE) was founded in 1976 when a group of African-American law enforcement officials attending a conference decided to address the high rate of crime in urban black communities and the economic conditions that lead to crime and violence. Subsequently NOBLE has evolved to encourage diversity at all levels of government; develop partnerships with communities in order to reduce violence and criminal activities; and address misconduct in law enforcement. NOBLE has been instrumental in establishing public policy and networks with other organizations addressing common concerns.

With more than thirty-eight chapters throughout the United States and a growing membership of 3,000 that includes police chiefs, sheriffs, and others who support their goals, NOBLE is noteworthy for its expertise in reporting research on criminal justice issues, developing training programs in cultural diversity, community partnerships, peer-exchange programs, and recruitment training. For further information contact:

NOBLE National Office
4609 Pinecrest Office Park Drive, Suite F
Alexandria, VA 22312-1442
(703) 658-1529

The National Sheriff's Association has more than 20,000 members including sheriffs, deputies, other law enforcement and public-safety professionals, and concerned citizens. Their goals are to inform members of emerging issues in law enforcement and to provide training and education programs.

Additionally members may enroll in benefit programs that include accidental death and dismemberment, discount registrations for affiliated conferences, and a subscription to *Sheriff Magazine.* To learn more contact:

National Sheriff's Association
1450 Duke Street
Alexandria, VA 22314-3490
(703) 836-7827

The Federal Law Enforcement Officers Association (FLEOA) represents officers working in federal law enforcement agencies. To be eligible to join you must be an active officer with any of more than seventy-four federal law enforcement agencies, a retiree of one of those agencies, or an associate member. The many benefits of FLEOA membership include representation by a legislative counsel who works on behalf of the membership on issues affecting federal law enforcement officers. Members also have access to twenty-four-hour legal services, should the need arise during the performance of their duties. FLEOA memberships are also honored by a number of businesses, including car rental and insurance, which offer discounts to members. For further information contact:

Federal Law Enforcement Officers Association
P.O. Box 508
East Northpoint, NY 11731-0472
(631) 368-6117

▦ THE SCENE OF THE CRIME

The American Academy of Forensic Sciences represents professionals such as criminologists, toxicologists, odontologists, document examiners, and others in the field of forensic science. Members receive benefits such as placement and referral services; seminars and meetings to develop forensic science skills; employment listings; and a subscription to the award-winning *Forensic Science Magazine*. To learn more contact:

American Academy of Forensic Science
410 North 21st Street, Suite 203
Colorado Springs, CO 80904-2798

■ THE COURTS

The American Bar Association (ABA) is an association for licensed lawyers that attempts to ensure the excellence and proper conduct of its members; helps members stay informed of recent developments in the ever-changing field of law; and sponsors continuing legal education opportunities, including courses at regional and national legal institutions, seminars, and videotapes. Members receive a variety of legal publications, including the *ABA Journal,* which chronicles the latest revisions and trends in law. ABA members also receive product and service discounts on telephone rates, hotels, and office equipment. To learn more contact:

American Bar Association
750 North Lake Shore Drive
Chicago, IL 60611
(312) 988-5000

Corrections

The American Jail Association (AJA) represents those who work in the nation's jails. AJA has approximately 4,800 members. Benefits include continuing education and training; updates on trends in the correctional and jail operation systems; the opportunity to network with peers; a subscription to *American Jails,* a bimonthly newsletter; and a complete listing of U.S. jails and jail administrators. Membership offers the opportunity for career enhancement through committee service; peer networking to develop alternative solutions for difficult situations; and discount registration for all AJA-sponsored training and conference sessions. For more information contact:

American Jail Association
2053 Day Road, Suite 100
Hagerstown, MD 21740
(301) 790-3930

Federal Bureau of Investigation Field Offices

22121 Eighth Avenue North, Room 1400
Birmingham, AL 35203
(205) 252-7705

One St. Louis Street
St. Louis Centre, 3rd Floor
Mobile, AL 36602
(205) 438-3674

101 East Sixth Avenue
Anchorage, AK 99501
(907) 276-4441

10825 Financial Center Parkway., Suite 200
Little Rock, AR 72211-3552
(501) 221-9100

201 East Indianola Avenue, Suite 400
Phoenix, AZ 85012
(602) 279-5511

11000 Wilshire Boulevard, Suite 1700
Los Angeles, CA 90024
(310) 477-6565

4500 Orange Grove Avenue
Sacramento, CA 95841
(916) 481-9110

9797 Aero Drive
San Diego, CA 92123-1800
(619) 565-1255

450 Golden Gate Avenue, 13th Floor
San Francisco, CA 94102-9523
(415) 553-7400

1961 Stout Street, Suite 1823
Denver, CO 80294
(303) 629-7171

150 Court Street, Room 535
New Haven, CT 06510
(203) 777-6311

7820 Arlington Expressway., Suite 200
Jacksonville, FL 32211
(904) 721-1211

16320 NW Second Avenue
Miami, FL 33169
(305) 944-9101

500 Zack Street, Room 610
Tampa, FL 33602
(813) 273-4566

2635 Century Parkway, NE, Suite 400
Atlanta, GA 30345
(404) 679-9000

Kalanianaole Federal Office Building, Room 4307
300 Ala Moana Boulevard
Honolulu, HI 96850
(808) 521-1411

E.M. Dirksen Federal Office Building, Room 905
219 South Dearborn Street
Chicago, IL 60604
(312) 431-1333

400 West Monroe Street, Suite 400
Springfield, IL 62704
(217) 522-9675

575 North Pennsylvania Street, Room 679
Indianapolis, IN 46204
(317) 639-3301

600 Martin Luther King Jr. Place, Room 500
Louisville, KY 40202
(502) 583-3941

1250 Poydras Street, Suite 2200
New Orleans, LA 70113-1829
(504) 522-4671

One Center Plaza, Suite 600
Boston, MA 02108
(617) 742-5533

7142 Ambassador Road
Baltimore, MD 21244-2754
(410) 265-8080

P.V. McNamara Federal Office Building, 26th Floor
477 Michigan Ave.
Detroit, MI 48226
(313) 965-2323

111 Washington Avenue S., Suite 1100
Minneapolis, MN 55401
(612) 376-3200

U.S. Courthouse, Room 300
811 Grand Avenue
Kansas City, MO 64106

L. Douglas Abram Federal Building, Room 2704
1520 Market Street
St. Louis, MO 63103
(314) 241-5357

100 W. Capitol Street, Room 1553
Jackson, MS 39269
(601) 948-5000

400 South Tyron Street, Suite 900
Charlotte, NC 28285

10755 Burt Street
Omaha, NE 68114
(402) 493-8688

One Gateway Center, 22nd Floor
Newark, NJ 07102-9889
(201) 622-5613

415 Silver Avenue, SW, Suite 300
Albuquerque, NM 87102
(505) 224-2000

700 E. Charleston Boulevard
Las Vegas, NV 89101
(702) 385-1281

James T. Foley Building, Suite 502
445 Broadway
Albany, NY 12207
(518) 465-7551

One FBI Plaza
Buffalo, NY 14202-2698
(716) 856-7800

315 Hudson Street, 2nd Floor
New York, NY 10278
(212) 335-2700

550 Main Street, Room 9023
Cincinnati, OH 45273-8501
(513) 421-4310

1240 East 9th Street, Room 3005
Cleveland, OH 44199-9912
(216) 522-1400

50 Penn Place, Suite 1600
Oklahoma City, OK 73118
(405) 842-7471

Crown Plaza Building
1500 SW First Avenue, Suite 401
Portland, OR 97201
(503) 224-4181

William J. Green Jr. Federal Office Building
600 Arch Street 8th Floor
Philadelphia, PA 19106
(215) 829-2700

U.S. Post Office Building
700 Grant Street, Suite 300
Pittsburgh, PA 15219
(412) 471-2000

U.S. Federal Building
150 Carlos Chardon Avenue, Room 526
Hato Rey
San Juan, PR 00918-1716
(809) 754-6000

1835 Assembly Street, Room 1357
Columbia, SC 29201
(803) 254-3011

John J. Duncan Federal Office Building
710 Locust Street, Suite 600
Knoxville, TN 37902
(423) 544-0751

Eagle Crest Building
225 N. Humphreys Boulevard, Suite 3000
Memphis, TN 38120-2017
(901) 747-4300

1801 North Lamar, Room 300
Dallas, TX 75202
(214) 720-2200

700 East San Antonio Avenue, Suite C-600
El Paso, TX 79901-7020
(915) 553-7451

2500 East TC Jester, Room 200
Houston, TX 77008-1300
(713) 868-2266

U.S. Post Office & Courthouse Building
615 E. Houston Street, Suite 200
San Antonio, TX 78205
(210) 225-6741

257 Towers Building, Suite 1200
257 East 200 South
Salt Lake City, UT 84111
(801) 579-1400

150 Corporate Boulevard
Norfolk, VA 23502
(804) 455-0100

111 Greencout Road
Richmond, VA 23228
(804) 261-1044

Tysons Corner
7799 Leesburg Pike, Suite 200
Falls Church, VA 22043
(703) 252-7801

915 Second Avenue, Room 710
Seattle, WA 98174-1096
(206) 622-0460

330 E. Kilbourn Avenue, Suite 600
Milwaukee, WI 53202-6627
(414) 276-4684

U.S. Customs Service Field Offices

555 East River Road
Tucson, AZ 85704
(520) 670-6026

300 South Ferry Street, Room 2037
Terminal Island, CA 90731
(310) 514-6231

185 West "F" Street, Suite 600
San Diego, CA 92101
(619) 744-4600

1700 Montgomery Street, Suite 445
San Francisco, CA 94111
(415) 705-4070

115 Inverness Drive East, Suite 300
Denver, CO 80112
(303) 784-6480

Scranton Building, 8075 NW 53rd Street
Miami, FL 33166
(305) 597-6030

2203 North Lois Avenue, Suite 600
Tampa, FL 33607
(813) 348-1881

1691 Phoenix Boulevard, Suite 250
Atlanta, GA 30349
(770) 994-2230

610 South Canal Street, Room1001
Chicago, IL 60607
(312) 353-8450

423 Canal Street, Room 210
New Orleans, LA 70130
(504) 589-6499

10 Causeway Street, Room 722
Boston, MA 02222
(617) 565-7400

200 St. Paul Place, Suite 2700
Baltimore, MD 21202
(410) 962-2620

McNamara Federal Building, Room 350
477 Michigan Avenue
Detroit, MI 48226-2568
(313) 226-3166

111 West Huron Street, Room 416
Buffalo, NY 14202
(716) 551-4375

6 World Trade Center, Room 714
New York, NY 10048
(212) 637-3900

#1 La Puntilla Street, Room 110
San Juan, PR 00901
(787) 729-6975

4141 N. Sam Houston Parkway East
Houston, TX 77032
(281) 985-0500

9400 Viscount Boulevard, Suite 200
El Paso, TX 79925
(915) 633-7200

10127 Morocco, Suite 180
San Antonio, TX 78216
(210) 229-4561

1000 2nd Avenue, Suite 2300
Seattle, WA 98104
(206) 553-7531

Contacts for Careers in Criminal Justice

▓ FEDERAL LAW ENFORCEMENT

U.S. Marshals Service

Human Resources Division
Field Support Team
600 Army Navy Drive
Arlington, VA 22202-4210
(202) 307-9437

U.S. Secret Service

1800 G Street, NW, Room 912
Washington, DC 20233
(202) 435-5800

Capitol Police

The U.S. Secret Service Uniformed Division/Recruitment
Office
1310 L Street NW, Suite 400

Washington, DC 20233
(202) 435-5800 or 1-800-827-7783

Drug Enforcement Agency

Office of Personnel, Recruitment, and Placement
400 Sixth Street SW, Room 2556
Washington, DC 20024
1-800-DEA-4288

Border Patrol

Contact the Telephone Application Process System:
(912) 757-3001

Bureau of Alcohol, Tobacco, and Firearms

U.S. Treasury Department
650 Massachusetts Avenue NW, Room 4170
Washington, DC 20226
(202) 927-8423

▓ MILITARY LAW ENFORCEMENT

U.S. Coast Guard Academy

Director of Admissions
15 Moehegan Avenue
New London, CT 06320-98008
1-800-424-8883 to inquire about enlistment or becoming
   a commissioned officer
1-800-GET-USCG to speak with a recruiter

Naval Criminal Investigative Service

Career Services Department
Washington Navy Yard, Building 11
716 Sicard Street SE
Washington, DC 20388-5380
(202) 433-3858

For civilian careers within military agencies contact:

Headquarters Human Resources Office
Undersecretary of the Navy
2211 South Clark Place
Arlington, VA 22244-5101

■ CORRECTIONS

Federal Bureau of Prisons

Mid-Atlantic Regional Office (Delaware, Indiana,
    Kentucky, Maryland, Michigan, North Carolina,
    Ohio, Tennessee, Virginia, West Virginia, and
    Washington, D.C.): (301) 317-3211.
North Central Regional Office (Colorado, Illinois, Iowa,
    Kansas, Minnesota, Missouri, Montana, Nebraska,
    North Dakota, South Dakota, Wisconsin, and
    Wyoming): (913) 551-1193.
Northeast Regional Office (Connecticut, Maine,
    Massachusetts, New Hampshire, New Jersey, New
    York, Pennsylvania, Rhode Island, and Vermont):
    1-800-787-2749.
South Central Regional Office (Arkansas, Louisiana,
    New Mexico, Oklahoma, and Texas):
    1-800-726-4473.

Southeast Regional Office (Alabama, Florida, Georgia, Mississippi, South Carolina, and Puerto Rico): (678) 686-1302.

Western Regional Office (Alaska, Arizona, California, Hawaii, Idaho, Nevada, Oregon, Utah, and Washington): (510) 803-5700.

COURT/LEGAL

American Association for Paralegal Education
P.O. Box 40244
Overland Park, KS 66204

National Association of Legal Assistants, Inc.
1601 South Main Street, Suite 300
Tulsa, OK 74119

National Court Reporters Association
8224 Old Courthouse Road
Vienna, VA 22182

COMPUTER SPECIALIST

Securities and Exchange Commission
6432 General Green Way
Alexandria, VA 22312
Attn: Personnel
(202) 942-4150

Web Site Directory

T HE FOLLOWING IS A SMALL SAMPLING OF SOME OF THE WEB
sites pertaining to criminal justice that were discovered
while researching this book. Posted by organizations or individuals, all offer quality information and many offer links to
other sites.

▓ THE FRONT LINES

Learn about the Los Angeles police: www.lapdonline.org
A site for California Tactical Officers (SWAT) that offers a
number of news stories among other information:
www.cactive.com/cato/
FBI official site: www.fbi.gov
ATF official site: www.atf/treas.gov/
DEA official site: www.usdoj.gov/dea/
Secret Service official site: www.treas.gov/usss
U.S. Treasury official site: www.treas.gov/uss
Securities and Exchanges Commission: www.sec.gov/

▤ THE SCENE OF THE CRIME

Details of famous crimes, criminals, and law enforcement officers: www.crimelibrary.com

Extensive information on criminal investigation and forensics: www.crimeandclues.com

"True Witness" forensics information: www.library.advanced.org/17049/

Forensic anthropology is discussed indepth at a professor's site: www.uncwil.edu/people/albertm/college.htm

Forensic entomology is described in detail at this very informative site: www.uio.no/~mostarke/forens_ent/introduction.shtml

American Society of Forensic Odontologists: www.ASFO.org.

Forensic psychology and psychiatry are reviewed in depth at "The Ultimate Forensic Psychology Database": www.flash.lakehead.ca/~pals/forensics/foren.htm

Follow the career of profiler Robert Kessler: www.robertkessler.com

Polygraph information: www.truthorlie.com/whatpoly.html

Polygraph information: www.soicc.huntingdon.edu/SOICC/LicOcc/polyexam.html

▤ THE COURTS

Information on the federal judiciary can be found at: www.bsc.edu/library/fed.jud.htm

State and federal courts: www.uscourts.gov/understanding_courts

U.S. Sentencing Commission: www.ussc.gov/overview.htm

■ CORRECTIONS

Ohio Department of Rehabilitation and Corrections:
www.dre.ohio.gov/web/ocac.htm
Nevada Corrections for Parole and Probations Officers:
www.aci.net/noyes/pnp/pptrain.html

■ PRIVATE SECURITY

Bounty Hunters Online: www.onworld.com/BHO/
To learn about the work of bodyguards:
www.professionalprotection.com